ABDULLAHI HAJI
My Life Through News Media

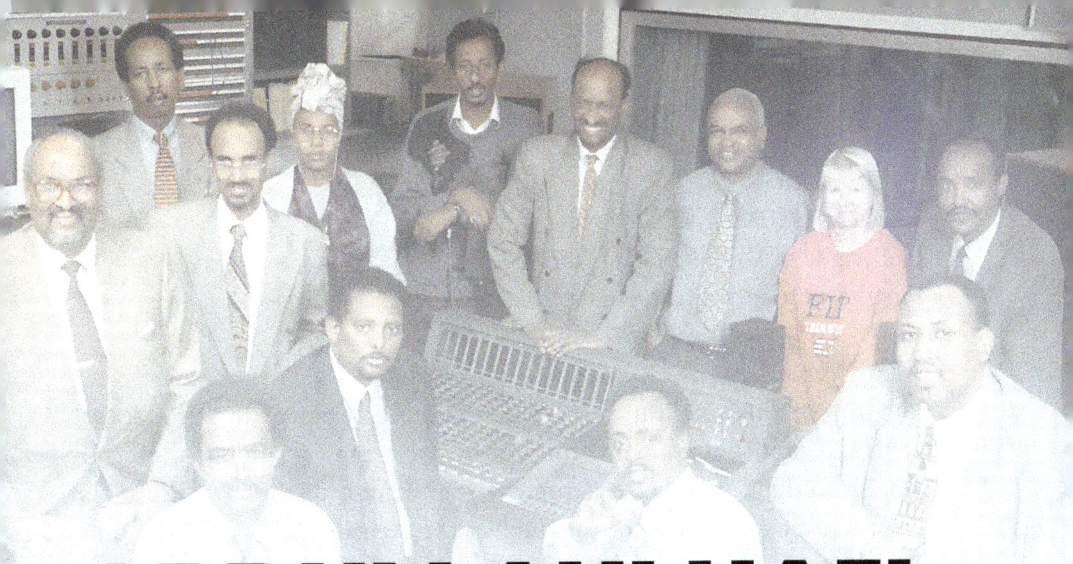

ABDULLAHI HAJI
MY LIFE THROUGH NEWS MEDIA

Editors
ABDISALAM M. ISSA-SALWE
AHMED SHEEKH MOHAMUD

LEICESTER | MOGADISHU
1447/2025

Looh Press LTD.
Copyright © Abdullahi Haji Abdi 2025
First Edition, First Print August 2025

All rights reserved.
No part of this publication may be reproduced, stored in any retrieval system, or transmitted in any form or by any means, including photocopying, recording, or other electronic or mechanical methods, without the prior written permission of the publisher, except in the case of brief quotations embodied in critical reviews and certain other non-commercial uses permitted by copyright law.

For permission and requests, write to the publisher or the author, at the address below.

PRINTED & DISTRIBUTED BY
Looh Press Ltd.
Leicester, England. UK
Mogadishu, Somalia
W: www.LoohPress.com
E: LoohPress@gmail.com
T: +44 79466 86693
T: +252 61 0743445 / +252 61 8707573

A catalogue record for this book is available from the British Library.
British Library Cataloguing-in-Publication Data

Editors	:	Abdisalam M. Issa-Salwe & Ahmed Sheikh Mohamud
Cover design & typeset	:	Kusmin (Looh Press)

ISBN:
978-1-912411-90-0 (Hardback)
978-1-912411-91-7 (Paperback)

CONTENTS

Dedication xi
Acknowledgments xiii
Forward xviii
Preface xxiii

PART ONE:
THE FOUNDATION YEARS 01

    CHAPTER 1: BRIEFLY ABOUT MY LIFE 03

PART TWO:
THE BBC SOMALI LANGUAGE 17

    CHAPTER 2: THE BBC SOMALI LANGUAGE 19

        2.4.1: Somalia's Proliferation of Communication Technology 23
        2.4.2: The Significance of the BBC's Influence On Somali Listeners 23
        2.4.3: The BBC Contribution to Somali Language 24
        2.4.4: Relocation of the BBC Somali Service 25

PART THREE:
SOMALIA'S MEDIA LANDSCAPE 28

    CHAPTER 3: THE IMPACT OF MEDIA ON SOCIETY 31

        3.4.1: Mass Communication Setting in Somalia 41
        3.4.2: The Influence of Mass Media 42
        3.4.3: The Power of The Impacts Phase of The Media 43
        3.5.1: Supporting the Somali Media Sector 47
        3.5.2: The Danger Zone 48
        3.5.3: Various News Sources 49
        3.6.1: The Future Prospect of Somali Social Media 49
        3.6.2: What Factors Increased Somali Media Such as Websites? 51

Contents

PART FOUR:
MANAGING INFORMATION 60

CHAPTER 4: ORAL CULTURE AND COMPUTER-MEDIATED COMMUNICATION 63

4.8.1: The Internet and Oral Qualities 64
4.8.2: Tendencies In Oral 65
4.8.3: Where Should We Go From Here? 66
4.8.4: Advocate for Regulatory Reform 67
4.8.5: Information Is High Demand Among the General Public 68
4.8.6: From Mass Media to Social Media 68
4.8.7: Influence Exerted by the Media 69
4.8.8: Making Use of Social Media 70
4.1.1: My Trip to Addis Ababa 73
4.2.1: Enforcement of the 1983 prohibition statute 83
4.3.1: The Case of Khat Between East African Nations 86
4.4.1: Kenyan Mira Khat 90
4.4.2: Khat Ban in Somalia 94
4.5.1: Yemeni khat from the town of Taiz 97
4.5.2: Here Is A Summary of It 97
4.5.3: A Debate On Khat Held In West London 98
4.5.4: My Speech on the Day I Was Receiving ISA 2019 Award: A Lifetime Achievement Awards 99
4.5.5: What I Have Emphasised 101

PART FIVE:
AWARDS & SPEECH 104

CHAPTER 5: A DISCOURSE ON KHAT TOOK PLACE IN WEST LONDON 107

5.7.1: My Scholarly Investigation: The Prohibition of Khat in Somalia 110

Bibliography 129
Index 133

DEDICATION

To the fearless voices of Somali journalism—

I dedicate this book to the journalists of the Somali people seeking the truth, shining light on the suppressed, and presenting it as true and as accurate as possible.

To those who asked the hard questions when silence was safer,

To those who paid the ultimate price for truth in the world's most dangerous profession,

To those who still broadcast hope from the ruins of war.

In memory of the colleagues we have lost,

In hope for the young voices yet to come.

This memoir belongs to every Somali journalist who understood that in our culture, to bear news is to bear the responsibility of keeping a scattered nation whole.

May your voices never be silenced.

ACKNOWLEDGMENTS

First and foremost I extend my heartfelt gratitude to Dr. Abdisalam M Issa-Salwe, vicechancellor and Professor of Information Management / Information Systems at East Africa University (Puntland, Somalia) and Amb. Ahmed Sheekh Mohamud (Professor of International Relations at East Africa University and Puntland State University, Puntland, Somalia). Their help has been invaluable in many ways and at many levels. They helped me organise decades of memories into a coherent narrative that honours both personal experiences and collective Somali history.

Another particular area is the way in which they helped extend my knowledge about modern technology in the news media. There have been many other individuals who made this memoir possible and supported my journey through the world of Somali broadcasting. First and foremost, I thank my sister Amina Haji and my uncle Haji Farah Haid, who raised me to become who I am now.

My deepest appreciation also goes to C.J. Martin, the former head of the BBC Somali Service. He recognised my potential and offered me an opportunity that defined my career. I also appreciate my BBC colleagues. I am deeply grateful to Jon Wilkins, head of the African BBC Service, who recognised the significance of my interview with President Siad Barre and honoured me with the first award given to a BBC staff member. Other colleagues whom I

Acknowledgments
ABDULLAHI HAJI ABDI

thank greatly include Mohamed Abdullahi, Hugh Walker, Patrick Gilkes, Yusuf Garaad Omar, and Abdirahman Abby Farah, and that moment validated not just my work but the importance of fearless journalism.

To the editors of this memoir, Abdisalam M. Issa-Salwe and Ahmed Sheekh Mohamud, thank you. Special recognition goes to the International Somali Awards committee, which honoured me with the 2019 Lifetime Achievement Award—which means everything comes from my own people.

Finally, I dedicate this work to the millions of Somalis worldwide who tuned in to their radios, seeking "warka"—news from home. You were not just my audience; you were my inspiration. In a culture where we greet each other with "ii waran" (tell me the news), I was privileged to be your voice across continents.

To future generations of Somali broadcasters and journalists: may you carry forward the responsibility of being truthful news bearers, for as our people say, "Warbaa ugu gaaja wayn" (information hunger is the worst hunger).

Abdullahi Haji Abdi
London, August 2025

FORWARD

MOHAMED ABDULLAHI,
FORMER HEAD OF BBC SOMALI SERVICE

A BIOGRAPHY OF THE VETERAN BROADCASTER ABDULLAHI HAJI IS LONG OVERDUE. I AM GLAD THAT TWO DISTINGUISHED SOMALI ACADEMICS, DR. ABDISALAM ISSA-SALWE AND AMBASSADOR AHMED SHEIKH, HAVE AT LAST HELPED WRITE THIS MUCH-NEEDED BOOK CHRONICLING THE CAREER OF A SOMALI MEDIA ICON. FRIENDS AND COLLEAGUES FONDLY KNOW HAJI AS A MAN OF IMMENSE TALENT. I WILL EXPLAIN THIS VIRTUE MORE FULLY A BIT LATER.

I have known Haji for nearly 50 years. In the 60s and 70s, I was part of his large and loyal audience. I started collaborating with Haji at the BBC in the early 1980s as a Nairobi-based correspondent. That is when our professional relationship began. On a weekly basis, he commissioned me to do reports for the BBC Somali Service and thereby guided me on reporting and editorial matters. I was surprised by his punctuality. If he said he would call at 2pm, expect the phone to ring at 2p.m. sharp. Expect as well that he would lick into shape your messy report. He would, however, congratulate you "for an excellent report." His eagle eye for editorial perfection is what, ten years later, I relied upon when I was appointed to head the BBC Somali Service.

I arrived in the Somali Service in 1993 when the Somali State had collapsed, and so had all institutions, including the state media

Forward
MOHAMED ABDULLAHI

outfits. As a result, the BBC became the sole national broadcaster for Somalis wherever they were located. That put an enormous burden on the service, broadening our remit beyond news, current affairs, and sports to providing a wholesome schedule, which should ideally be provided by local media and by stations that have ample broadcasting hours. (Initially, the BBC Somali Service broadcast for one hour per day, which was later expanded by an extra half an hour.) For instance, we had to provide emergency services, including disaster alerts. The presence of warring factions complicated our work.

Earlier, I said Haji is a man of immense talent, as he has many excellent character traits, but I will limit myself to a handful. Discipline and a sterling work ethic: on retirement from the BBC after 30 years of service, he had missed work for four days on sick leave. (After retirement, his services were needed by the BBC as a parttimer for many years). That's not to say he didn't fall ill at other times, but he consistently showed up for work despite his illness. He was never known to be late for work or for any other appointment. We all knew that any task given to him would be completed in perfection. As an expert Somali speaker, Haji has contributed to the advancement of the Somali language by coining words and phrases to translate new foreign vocabularies and technological innovations. Apart from Somali, Haji speaks fluent Amharic, English, and German. This has enabled him to domesticate for his audiences difficult foreign concepts and ideas. He has a solid background in world history and politics, which enables him to provide informed analysis of issues at hand.

Haji has always been trusted to provide guidance on the recruitment of new staff. During the period I headed the service, not a single appointment was made without Haji›s approval. I trusted his recommendations. He had a deep understanding of the Somali media scene. And he was always fair. His decisions were always guided by his respect for talent and ability. Politicians sometimes complained about his robust interviewing methods. What surprised me was that even his detractors would always request Haji to interview them.

I could say a great deal of good about Haji, but that would make this preface too long. Even then, I have to say one final virtue: Haji is beyond reproach when it comes to financial matters. Many attempts were made by Somali governments and individuals, but he declined all those dirty offers. I have concrete evidence in this regard.

I hope this book will benefit many readers and guide us in emulating Haji.

Mohamed Abdullahi
Former Head of BBC Somali Service.
Nairobi, Kenya
August, 2025

Forward
MOHAMED ABDALLAHI

FORWARD

AMBASSADOR YUSUF GARAAD OMAR
FORMER HEAD OF BBC SOMALI SERVICE (2000-2012)

Abdullahi Haji's voice ranks among the most distinguished, if not the most recognisable, in Somali broadcasting. I have been listening to his work since I first became aware of journalism, and he was among the earliest reporters I encountered, alongside notable figures such as Yaasiin Haji Ismail Jirde, Abdi Haji Gobdoon, and Ahmed Ali Askar. I first made contact with Abdullahi Haji by telephone in 1991, when I joined the BBC World Service Somali Section as a reporter based in Italy. Following the collapse of the Somali government, the majority of Somalis who fled to Europe settled in Italy, including former political leaders, military personnel, business figures, members of the judiciary, and community leaders. Regular flights continued to arrive weekly from Somalia, maintaining this connection.

IMAGE 26:
From left to right, the author Abdulahi Haji, and Yusuf Garaad
London, 2025.
Courtesy of Yusuf Garaad

Forward
AMBASSADOR YUSUF GARAAD OMAR

Since the BBC had no correspondent in Mogadishu at that time and telephone communications had been severed, Nairobi and Rome became the two primary stations providing the most comprehensive coverage of Somali affairs. Haji consistently provided me with guidance on sensitive stories, given his position as the only Senior Producer in the service. His role within the team extended beyond that of a conventional Senior Producer, as both the Head of Service and Deputy Head did not speak Somali and relied entirely upon his editorial judgement.

When President George H.W. Bush announced from the White House on Friday, 4th December 1992, that he would deploy more than 25,000 marines to Somalia, the BBC planned to expand its morning programming. The Deputy Head of Section, Denis Benton, contacted me to offer a six-month contract in London. Given that I was studying at two universities whilst maintaining both a scholarship and employment, I initially hesitated. Haji spoke with me extensively and persuaded me to accept the offer.

Subsequently, Abdullahi Haji and I worked together for twenty years, undertaking joint assignments, conducting recruitment interviews for new BBC staff, and delivering training programmes together. He gained recognition for conducting challenging interviews, though perhaps his most significant legacy lies in his contributions to Somali linguistic development. He enriched the Somali language with new terminology and participated in collaborative efforts to create Somali glossaries. I recall that the term "geeddi-socodka nabadda" (peace process) was among the expressions he introduced. Live broadcasting demands considerable skill under pressure. Abdullahi Haji approached his work with exceptional seriousness, maintained punctuality, and consistently met all deadlines leading to live programmes.

I have always known Abdullahi Haji to be an intensely private and reserved individual. His social interactions, dining habits, dress code, transportation arrangements, and scheduling all followed established routines. When I last met him in West London in August 2025, I observed no change in his characteristic elegance, cleanliness, and dignified bearing. Abdullahi Haji consistently maintained an elegant appearance, demonstrating meticulous attention to personal grooming and dress. I cannot recall ever seeing him without a tie. He greeted people with a cheerful countenance and ready smile. He is a man of few words but profound respect and consideration for others. He listened attentively and spoke concisely, ensuring his words carried substantial meaning.

Furthermore, he actively encouraged his colleagues and readily assisted those requiring support. He rarely encountered anyone without offering some form of compliment or positive observation. His daily routine included reading newspapers and following international news on radio and television programming. Among the programmes he watched religiously were Question Time and Panorama.

As I served as Head of the Somali Section during his final day, he departed quietly from the thirty-year career he had maintained without ceremony, carrying only boxes containing correspondence, cassettes and press cuttings. He even declined my offer to arrange a taxi for his departure. I accompanied him outside the building as a courtesy, watching as he made his way toward the nearest tube station. In that quiet moment, I found myself reflecting deeply.

As to this autobiography represents a remarkable journey through the evolution of modern Somali media and journalism. Through Abdullahi Haji's eyes, we witness not merely a personal career trajectory, but the entire transformation of how the Somali people connected with their homeland and each other during the most turbulent period of their modern history. His story illuminates the profound responsibility borne by those who carry news to a people for whom information has always been survival itself.

What makes this narrative particularly compelling is its demonstration of journalism as both craft and calling. Haji's meticulous attention to detail, his unwavering punctuality, and his commit-

Forward
AMBASSADOR YUSUF GARAAD OMAR

ment to accuracy reflect professional standards that transcended the chaos surrounding him. His linguistic innovations, including coining terms like "geeddi-socodka nabadda" (peace process), as I have mentioned earlier, show how journalists shape not just understanding but language itself. For anyone in media, communications, or public service, his example provides a masterclass in maintaining integrity under pressure whilst remaining deeply connected to one's audience.

> Haji's story offers invaluable insights into the intersection of technology, culture, and diaspora experience. Haji's career spans the golden age of radio through the emergence of digital media, capturing how technological shifts reshape entire societies. His analysis of khat's social impact, drawn from both journalistic observation and personal experience, provides a nuanced examination of cultural practices that resist simple categorisation.

Through Haji's experience, we see how radio journalism can dismantle barriers once considered unbreakable.

During Somalia's darkest hours, when state institutions collapsed and communities fractured, Haji and his colleagues at the BBC Somali Service became the invisible threads holding a scattered nation together. Their voices carried not just news, but hope, identity, and continuity. This is essential reading for anyone seeking to understand the power of media to heal, inform, and unite—demonstrating that in skilled hands, journalism becomes both witness to history and guardian of human dignity..

Ambassador Yusuf Garaad Omar
Former Head of BBC Somali Service (2000-2012)
London, England
August, 2025

PREFACE

WE, AS THE EDITORS OF THE WORK OF ABDULLAHI HAJI, THANK HIM FOR GIVING US THE OPPORTUNITY TO WORK ON HIS MEMORIES. WRITING THE LIFE AND MEMORIES OF AN IMPORTANT PERSON, SUCH AS ABDULLAHI HAJI, IS AN EXTREMELY HONOURABLE TASK BECAUSE IT LETS US EXTEND OUR NAME AND HONOUR.

It is long past time for a biography of legendary broadcaster Abdullahi Haji, who has been working at the BBC Somali Service for 36 years. Haji is a well-known person and a man of extraordinary talent.

Abdullahi Haji is well respected by the BBC Somali Service, as we have noted that all the old and new staff have provided us good information about Abdullahi Haji. During our research of Abdullahi Haji, we have found that all those we were interviewing were very happy and congratulating us for the work of the memoir of Abdullahi Haji.

It was an honour and privilege for us to write the history of Abdullahi Haji. The name and honour are born from Abdullahi's stature as the longest-serving person on the BBC Somali Service.

In fact, every work that is done has difficult beginnings, or its direction is difficult to find. Furthermore, at the beginning it was a difficult task for us to find complete information and information about Abdullahi Haji.

The unfortunate thing was that when we contacted the BBC, we found out that the old history of the BBC Somali service had disappeared from its documents. This forced us to contact the BBC staff and executives to conduct various interviews.

Preface
DR ABDISALAM M ISSA-SALWE AND AMB. AHMED SHEEKH MOHAMUD (EDS.)

Thank you to the former BBC staff and executives for helping us by providing us with a lot of information about Abdullahi Haji.

At last we have been successful in compiling and creating the current work.

We hope that the path taken by Abdullahi Haji will serve as an example for many people and that they will follow this valuable path that has gone down in history. This book will definitely be useful for the future generation, providing them with a way to emulate Abdullahi Haji and become contributors to the development of modern communication media.

Dr Abdisalam M Issa-Salwe and Amb. Ahmed Sheekh Mohamud (*eds.*)
London, England
August, 2025

Abdullahi Haji
MY LIFE THROUGH NEWS MEDIA

CHAPTER 1

BRIEFLY ABOUT MY LIFE

1.1: INTRODUCTION

I was born in Warder on 15 October 1939. When I was six years old (in 1945), my sister Amina Haji came to where my father was living with a significant number of livestock, which was not very far from the town of Dhagahbur.

My sister asked my father to allow her to take me with her to Dhagahbur and to enrol me with a school. My father agreed to allow me to go with my sister to Dhagahbur. After a night journey of seven hours, we arrived in Dhagahbur and stayed with my auntie, Osob Mohamed Hayd. After a few days my sister took me to enrol me in the Sheikh Sufi Quranic school.

After seven months my sister took me to the town of Harar and handed me over to my uncle Haji Farah Hayd, who was a rich

Part One
The Foundation Years

businessman. After a few days, my uncle enrolled me in a preschool to learn the Amharic language. In Ethiopia, Amharic was the main language at the time. The Amharic language was the official language of Ethiopia (70-plus languages are spoken in Ethiopia).

It was also an opportunity to build the future with knowledge of the language. After nearly a year, the school transferred me to Haile Selassie Intermediate School in Harar.

I studied at that school for about seven years, and then I was ready to go to secondary school. Because I excelled at school, I gained a lot of experience and valuable knowledge.

Consequently, the school attracted a substantial student body. I also had the opportunity to be one of the students.

After a few years, a team from the Ethiopian Air Force occasionally visited the school to select students. They came from a military base called Bishoftu (or Debrezet).

I applied for the pilot training programme. I was fortunate enough to secure an interview slot. One of the questions they asked me was to name some of the world's renowned writers. I was lucky to answer that the most renowned writers were Shakespeare and Dickens.

I successfully answered all the questions, demonstrating my proficiency. I, along with around ten students, successfully completed the test, which led to us being selected for the training. A few days later, they took us to Bishoftu for the training.

One day during the training, the head of the training department called us to ask which department we would like to go to. I answered that I wanted to become a pilot.

1.2: THE BUILDING OF MY CAREER

After two months of training, the late Emperor Haile Selassie of Ethiopia visited the camp where I received it. Emperor Haile Selassie likes to visit training centres, and Bishoftu was one of the locations he used to visit.

He used to ask students questions like, «What are you learning?»

That afternoon, we waited in line for the king. The emperor was accompanied by a number of military officers, including generals and colonels.

I was in the middle of the queue. The emperor came in front of me by asking, "And you, what are you learning?" I answered, "Your Majesty, I want to become a pilot, so I will fly aeroplanes." Then, he said to me, "Do you really want to become a pilot and try to fly aeroplanes?" I answered, "Yes, your Majesty, I want to become a pilot and try to fly aeroplanes."

His Majesty said, "Are you really sure you want to become a pilot? You're too young to handle aeroplanes."

His Majesty saw me as a thin and very young man, and he believed that my age prevented me from handling an aeroplane. He believed that I was wasting my time, as I was incapable of handling or flying an aeroplane. Then I replied that flying an aeroplane does not require physical strength. Flying aeroplanes requires skills and intelligence.

The emperor looked at me with sharp eyes, and he moved away without saying anything else to me.

There was a rule that forbade people to answer to the emperor. The custom was to simply respond with "Yes, king" only. After a few minutes, one of the officers approached me and informed me that I should never answer to the emperor.

I started worrying about my future in the camp because of the way the emperor looked at me as I answered his questions sharply and the way the officers told me that I was never supposed to answer him. I was worried that I might never have the opportunity to continue my training and they might transfer me to the air force as a cadet instead of letting me become a pilot.

I submitted a request to be released from the training school, as I felt it would be difficult for me to continue the pilot programme.

Fortunately, the training camp released me after a few weeks. So I went back to Harar to stay at my uncle's house. My uncle was shocked

Part One
The Foundation Years

that I left the Air Force training. He said that the pilot training was supposed to be important and beneficial for me. I informed him about the emperor's questions, observations, and the manner in which I addressed them. I discovered that it was improper for me to respond to his questions. So, although I continued the training, my worries increased about losing the opportunity to become a pilot.

After staying with my uncle, I applied to be admitted to Ambo Agricultural College. Ambo is located north of Addis Ababa. Fortunately, the college accepted my application.

I studied for two years. After some time, my uncle returned to the college to tell me about an opportunity at Addis Ababa Radio. He asked me if I wanted to apply for that job. In response, I told him that I wanted to work as a broadcaster. Becoming a broadcaster was also one of my dreams.

My uncle took me to Addis Ababa's Ministry of Information. At the Ministry of Information, I was given the opportunity to participate in an interview and take a test. Abdullahi Abdi, a Somali broadcaster of the Addis Ababa radio, led the test.

Abdullahi Abdi used to translate the Somali news, using the Amharic alphabet. He advised me to use the Amharic alphabet as he was doing.

As the Somali script was not yet written in that period, it was difficult for me to translate the Somali news using the Amharic alphabet. I have been at Addis Ababa Radio for about three years.

In 1963, I found a broadcasting and journalism scholarship from Germany. So I left for Germany. The Minister of Information informed me that the king would provide guidance on studying abroad. I had another opportunity to meet the emperor.

In this period, the emperor asked me if I was going to Germany. I replied that I was indeed going to Germany. He asked me how long I would be studying in Germany. I replied that the study will take me a year and a half.

Then he asked me, «Is it possible that tomorrow you may say that I am from Mogadishu?"

At that time, I had no intention of visiting Somalia or any place apart from Ethiopia. I said to the emperor, "How could a proud subject like me leave his emperor and country? I will never go to another country. This is my country, and I am proud to be in Ethiopia." The emperor waved his head and said, "We shall see it."

The next day, I flew to Cologne, Germany, to attend my scholarship. At that time, Germany was divided into East and West. The east was the communist part, while the west was in the capitalist part. I started studying broadcasting in Cologne. I was there for one and a half years. Then I returned to Ethiopia after finishing my studies.

The next day, I went to see the minister and asked him if he would inform the emperor that I had returned to Addis Ababa after completing my studies in Germany. The minister replied that he would not disclose anything to the emperor and that it was my responsibility to continue with my tasks.

I continued to work from 1964 until 1967. At the end of 1967, there was a new minister at the Ministry of Information, and I applied to be sent to London to pursue further training in journalism. My request has been accepted, and after a few weeks, I fly to London to start my training.

After a few months I went to the BBC Somali Service and met the head of the BBC Somali Service, Mr. C. J. Martin. After I introduced myself to him, I said that I am a radio broadcaster from Addis Ababa. I told him that I had travelled to London to receive training in broadcasting and that I have many years of radio experience.

I expressed my desire to be connected with the BBC Somali Service and my willingness to join them as a professional broadcaster should a job vacancy arise. He promised me that if there was a vacancy, he would contact me.

After a few weeks I went back to see Mr. C. J. Martin, and I told him that I will go to Germany again for another training. I told

Part One
THE FOUNDATION YEARS

him that I was familiar with Germany because I had previously been there for broadcasting training. I gave him my address in Germany, and he promised to contact me if there was an opportunity to work with the BBC.

At the end of 1969, I received a letter from Mr. C. J. Martin stating that there was a vacancy in the BBC Somali service. He was asking me if I would be willing to join the service.

I was pleased to reply immediately that I was glad to accept the offer. I packed my bags quickly, and I flew to London.

It was on November 22, 1969, when I joined the BBC. I attended four weeks of induction courses, as the training covered the workings of the BBC, its various departments, and other crucial information about the service.

I had the opportunity to meet colleagues at the service, including Hussein Mohamed Bullale, Osman Hassan, Osman Sugulle, and many others. Additionally, students from Somalia used to come to work as part-timers. They were not permanent, as they were given broadcasting training.

Since I came from Ethiopia, my new colleagues used to refer to me as 'habashi.' They used to joke about me being an Amhar (Ethiopian). Politically, Somalis used to despise Ethiopians, and anyone from Ethiopia used to receive insulting and occasionally offensive remarks.

During that period, there were some hostilities between Somalia and Ethiopia, following the colonial power's takeover of part of the Somali-inhabited territories and giving them to Ethiopia.

The BBC had a rule that mandated a three-year probation period for new staff. Similarly, the new workers would receive a one-month break or holiday after three years. Following the break, the new staff would receive two more years of working contracts.

At the BBC Somali service, there were no permanent contracts. Everything was based on a temporary contract. I continued working for five years.

Abdullahi Haji
My Life Through News Media

In 1972 I was given an assignment to go to Mogadishu to collect material for the BBC Somali service.

At that time, the military had been in power for two years after overthrowing the civilian government in October 1969. The military formed a Supreme Revolutionary Council (SRC), which was led by General Mohamed Siyad Barre.

Before I went to Mogadishu, my colleagues advised me to be careful with the new military regime.

After some time, I attempted to arrange an interview with the president. I have been waiting for a week, and at last the president accepted my request to interview him.

I went to the president's office, and the staff president instructed me to wait until the president was ready to receive me for the interview.

I have been instructed to wait at the presidential reception. Unfortunately, I stayed at the reception for many hours, and I became tired and slept.

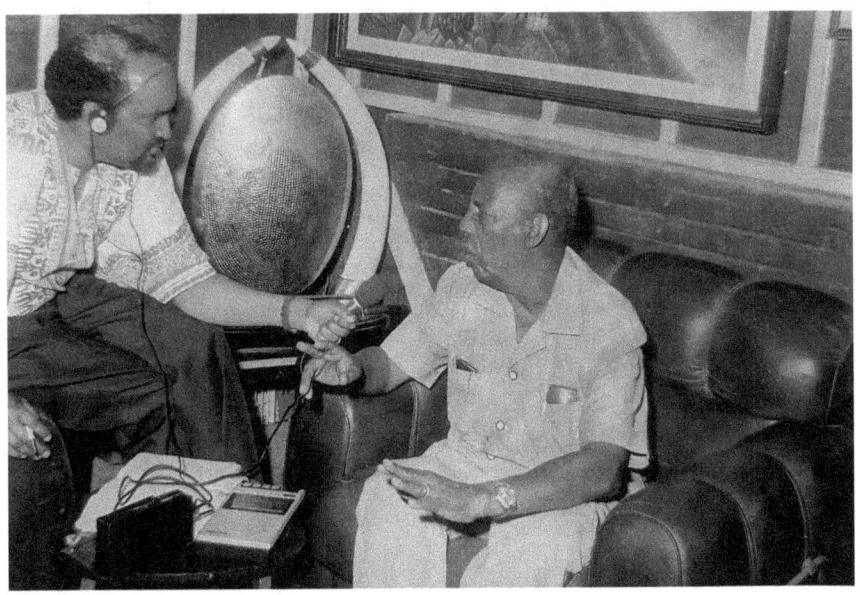

IMAGE 12:
From left to right: the author Abdulahi Haji, the then Somali President Mohamed Siad Barre.

Part One
THE FOUNDATION YEARS

IMAGE 13:

From left to right: the author Abdulahi Haji, Abdirahman Jama Barre, and President Mohamed Siad Barre.

The president used to stay awake until late in the night. Latenight the staff called me to go to the president's room for the interview.

I felt a bit dishevelled and confused due to my tiredness. But fortunately, I had my questions written on a paper. My first question was this:

> "My president, as you have overthrown the civilian government and the Somalis are not familiar with military rule, when will you go back to your barracks and give the rule to the civilian government?"

The question shocked the president, as it was a question he had never been expecting. He stared at me with a menacing view. Nevertheless, he was composed and confident. So he started answering my question by saying,

"Listen to me very clearly: We aren't concerned about who wears a military uniform or civilian cloth. But we care about people who can do something good for the country."

His words were like a bombshell, and he clearly expressed that the military rule was necessary.

After completing my interview, I immediately prepared to travel to London for the broadcast of that interview. I was aware that the BBC Somali Service would be paying close attention to my interview.

I edited the tape and prepared it for broadcast. My colleagues have responded positively to my interview with the head of the Somali military coup.

The interview was translated into many languages. The most popular moment in the interview was my question, «When will you return to your military barracks?»

John Wilkinson, Head of the African BBC Service, who honoured me with the a unique award never given any staff before a BBC staff member. The award validated not only my work but also the importance of fearless journalism.

I have been given £75. At that time, seventy-five British pounds represented a significant amount of money. The gift was a first for a BBC staff member.

The interview strengthened my profession and my reputation as a broadcaster. The impact of the interview has also resulted in Somalis around the world purchasing radios to follow the BBC Somali news services. People became curious to follow what was going on in Somalia.

1.3: THE POWER OF THE MASS MEDIA AND ITS GLOBAL

My life commenced when the world transitioned to utilising radio as a form of mass media rather than relying on contemporary information technology, such as the internet, commonly referred to today as social media. Media exerts a significant influence globally.

Part One
THE FOUNDATION YEARS

The rapidity of communication via electronic media reflects what McLuhan described as "the speed of the senses" (McLuhan, 1964) within his concept of the 'Global Village'. We are now able to hear and observe events occurring thousands of miles away within seconds.

CNN provided remarkable live coverage of the millennium celebration, originating from Chatham Island in the Pacific, where the first millennium clock struck. The event showcased global interconnectedness. The advancements in communication technology allowed this initiative to be realised.

Following the disintegration of the Somali state in the early 1990s, the BBC, which previously provided daily broadcasts in Somali, has emerged as a crucial source of news and information for Somalis in the Horn of Africa.

The Somali nomad places significant importance on information. Constant awareness of one's surroundings is essential for survival in a challenging environment. This approach has encouraged Somalis to actively pursue information.

Issa-Salwe (1996) indicates that Somali nomads rely on accurate knowledge to navigate their surroundings, manage livestock, and access resources in a challenging, arid region, underscoring the critical role of information in their survival and well-being. It impacts a wide range of areas, from traditional crafts such as weaving to modern challenges like access to healthcare, shaping their lifestyle, social frameworks, and cultural practices.

In oral societies, the act of avoiding information equates to distancing oneself from the community as a whole. Samatar, 1996 According to Professor Said Samatar, the English greeting "How are you?" has a minimum of eight Somali equivalents. The English version focuses on inquiring about the recipient's well-being, whereas the Somali version seeks to gather information regarding various aspects, including the surrounding area and the community, among others. (Ibid.).

In modern technology, ICTs hold significant importance for Somalis, whose culture is predominantly oral. The impact of this situation was particularly notable during the civil unrest that began in early 1991, which led to the collapse of the nation's infrastructure and resulted in citizens being deprived of essential services.

During the initial years of the International Red Cross's operation, individuals were able to send letters or notes to their relatives worldwide, facilitated by postal services established across Somalia and refugee centres in neighbouring countries. In a similar vein, the BBC Somali service in London initiated a Missing Relative Session (Olden, 1999) that allows individuals to submit their enquiries via mail. Two times daily, the service broadcasts in Somali.

1.4: THE BEGINNING ROLE AS RADIO BROADCASTER-MY YEARS WITH RADIO ETHIOPIA

I commenced my career in broadcasting in the 1950s with Ethiopian radio. I commenced with the initiation of the expansion of the BBC World Service. The Somali language branch was established in the 1950s, and I had the privilege of being part of the team at the BBC's Somali language branch.

In the late 1950s, I commenced my career as a broadcaster for the BBC Somali Service. The British Broadcasting Corporation (BBC) stands out as the largest and most esteemed broadcasting system globally. The BBC Somali Service is widely regarded as the benchmark for excellence among Somali-speaking communities worldwide. I consistently emphasised engaging with the BBC's daily programmes.

Focusing on the radio box could lead to a significant stagnation in adult life. In the 1950s, I became a dedicated listener of the Somali Service, as it was the sole source of Somali-speaking radio programming available at the time.

The extensive and comprehensive daily coverage of global news; the traditional yet occasionally innovative vocabulary;

Part One
The Foundation Years

and, most notably, the engaging voices of the broadcasters, who skilfully blended a relaxed tone with clarity suitable for the specific programme or news item, were all defining features. I became involved in those tasks, and it was a valuable experience that improved my broadcasting skills.

I joined the team charged with preparing highly sensitive programmes, including interviews with notable figures. These tasks served as the foundational elements of my skill development.

The BBC commenced its radio broadcasts in 1922, maintaining original authority over the airwaves. Nonetheless, the radio broadcasts continue to be produced as a vital component of the corporation's output in the present day. Although the UK did not issue any additional broadcasting licences until 1973, foreign commercial competitors began to emerge shortly thereafter. Somali The BBC News narrative is in the early 1960s, a period marked by the Somali people's quest for independence from colonial rule. (BBC, 18 October 1922)

I began my broadcasting career at the Ethiopian radio station. The BBC commenced its radio broadcasts in 1922. The General Post Office of the British Government, which initially managed the airwaves, issued licences to the BBC, as the law previously considered them an extension of Post Office services. Radio broadcasts continue to represent a substantial segment of the corporation's output today, as reflected in the BBC listings. This format represents the cornerstone of contemporary mass media communication technology.

In 1932, the corporation introduced the BBC Empire Service on shortwave, starting with English programming and rapidly expanding to include other languages, thereby providing a unique service separate from that of the domestic audience. Following the onset of World War II, the corporation rebranded its Overseas Service, which is now known as the BBC World Service.

According to Marshall McLuhan (1964), communication media serve as an extension of the senses, and the "sensory balance" of individuals within a society impacts their level of awareness. Meyrowitz argues that the media establishes a "new social environment" that operates independently of an individual's physical presence or geographical location.

The functional relevance and consequences of older media, including oral messaging, letter writing, and taped transmissions, have evolved in Somalia due to the advent of the telephone and other communication technologies.

In the late 1950s, it was the Italians in Mogadishu who pioneered the establishment of radio communications. Guglielmo Marconi, the individual who oversaw the radio station communications in the capital of Italian Somalia, was also responsible for the first radio station messages across the entire continent of Africa. In 1938, Guglielmo Marconi launched a public radio service in the Italian language, initially focused on broadcasting within the Mogadishu-Genale-Villa Abbruzzi area

Part Two:
The BBC Somal

anguage

Part Two
THE BBC SOMALI LANGUAGE

CHAPTER 2

THE BBC SOMALI LANGUAGE

The BBC Somali Service operates as a radio station within the BBC World Service framework. The service is broadcast in the Somali language, initially established its headquarters at Broadcasting House in West London, and relocated its Somali service to Nairobi in 2012.

The majority of the audience members are located in the Horn of Africa and the surrounding regions. The station functions as a crucial connection between individuals residing in Somalia and those located in various regions globally.

Part Two
THE BBC SOMALI LANGUAGE

The station was established on July 18, 1957, with two weekly programmes, each lasting fifteen minutes. In September 1958, the station commenced daily broadcasting. On July 1, 1961, two segments of the programmeme were merged, resulting in an extension of the programmeme's duration to thirty minutes. Since that time, the frequency of broadcasts has increased.

The existing schedule includes three half-hour programmes and one hour-long show that are aired daily. The station is actively engaged in developing local networks in all Somali-speaking regions worldwide, encompassing Somalia, Djibouti, the Somali region of Ethiopia, and Northeastern Kenya, along with the Somali diaspora in various African nations. An article published on AllAfrica.com in August 2010 indicates that Shabelle Media Network has begun broadcasting a selection of the station's programmes.

2.1: BBC HISTORY

On July 18, 1957, the station launched with two weekly programs, each with a duration of fifteen minutes. In September 1958, the station commenced daily broadcasting. On July 1, 1961, the station merged the two segments of the program, extending its length to thirty minutes. Since that time, the frequency of broadcasts has increased. The station broadcasts three half-hour programs and one hour-long show each day as part of its schedule.

Additionally, the station has been actively engaged in developing local networks in all Somali-speaking regions worldwide, encompassing Somalia, Djibouti, Ethiopia, and Northeastern Kenya, along with the Somali diaspora in various African nations. In August 2010, AllAfrica.com published an article indicating that Shabelle Media Network had commenced broadcasting a selection of the station's programs.

2.2: THE FOUNDATION OF MODERN COMMUNICATION TECHNOLOGY

In 1932, the corporation introduced the BBC Empire Service on shortwave, starting with English programming and rapidly expanding to include other languages, such as Somali, to provide a unique service tailored to an international audience. In response to the outbreak of World War II, the corporation rebranded its service as the Overseas Service, which is now recognised as the BBC World Service.

Individuals perceive radio media as an enhancement of their sensory experiences, and their "sensory equilibrium" within a community influences their level of awareness. The media establishes a "new social environment" that operates independently of an individual's physical presence or geographical location. The functional relevance and consequences of older media, including oral messaging, letter writing, and taped transmissions, have evolved in Somalia due to the advent of the telephone and other communication technologies.

Individuals perceive communication media, such as radio waves, as an extension of their sensory experience and contend that a person's "sensory balance" within a culture affects their consciousness level. Researchers have highlighted the concept that media creates a "new social environment" that operates independently of an individual's physical presence or location. The functional relevance and consequences of older media, including oral messaging, letter writing, and taped transmissions, have evolved in Somalia due to the advent of the telephone and other communication technologies.

2.3: BBC AS PART OF EVERYDAY SOMALI NEWS

Issa-Salwe (2008) affirms this. The media is of paramount importance to the Somali Diaspora in Somalia, as it serves a multifaceted and essential function. It functions as a critical source of information, a means of preserving cultural identity, and a platform for political expression and engagement.

One could contend that Somalia's society is among the most media-literate in Africa. A common language and an enduring love of poetry unite this severely divided, war-torn, and presently drought- and famine-stricken nation, despite all of its divisions.

2.4: RADIO MOGADISHU

Radio Mogadishu was founded in 1951, during Somalia's time under United Nations trusteeship and Italian control, the former colonial power. It initially commenced the dissemination of news in Italian, followed shortly by the broadcasting of content in Somali. UNSOM, October 21, 2023

Radio Mogadishu, the public broadcasting entity, was managed by the colonial administration. Broadcasting began in 1951 under the name Radio Mogadishu, initially providing news programmes in Somalia and Italy. In 1960, the Russian government enhanced the station to facilitate domestic service in Somali, Amharic, and Oromo, subsequent to the country's independence.

The national broadcaster's expansion and development over the following three decades were abruptly interrupted in 1991 due to the outbreak of civil war in Somalia. The ousting of Somalia's then-president, Siyad Barre, led to the cessation of operations at Radio Mogadishu shortly thereafter. Competing factions gained control of the station due to its strategic geographic location.

In the 1993 skirmishes involving a faction and foreign troops in the city, the archives incurred damage. This information is sourced from the United Nations Sustainable Development Group report dated 13 February 2024. A significant part of Somalia's cultural heritage was destroyed by the violence that affected the nation. The museums either destroyed the objects or sold them on the illicit market following their removal from the collections. The archives of Radio Mogadishu were specifically targeted, and the records of Somali National TV were destroyed in the attack.

2.4.1: Somalia's Proliferation of Communication Technology

With the exception of telecommunications, Somalia has neglected nearly all other development initiatives since the onset of the civil war. The telecom industry, which encompasses fax machines and mobile phones, has expanded throughout the Somali territory.

This entrepreneurial expansion is driven by the Somali people's insatiable desire for knowledge and communication. For instance, Somali entrepreneurs were motivated to enter the global telephone industry by the significant demand for communication technologies. In London, Somali entrepreneurs operate thirty phone booths that provide low-cost international calls, phone cards, mobile phones, and other connected products.

The number of Somali social media and correspondence lists has experienced a substantial increase recently. Compared to the conventional Somali communication pattern, this novel mode of communication illustrates the influence of change. The new communication technology is primarily employed by the Somali Diaspora and professionals to maintain contact, remain organised, and contribute to the restoration of their homelands.

2.4.2: The Significance of the BBC's Influence On Somali Listeners

The founders of the BBC believed that broadcasting had the capacity to improve socioeconomic conditions. Public intervention has the potential to provide individuals with knowledge, culture, and information; strengthen communities; and initiate a dialogue about identity and the future for the benefit of the public.

Part Two
THE BBC SOMALI LANGUAGE

Their establishment and support facilitated the development of a diverse array of programmes. This new cultural institution has established a dynamic that has contributed to the enhancement of public value, as it is committed to the highest standards of excellence, integrity, impartiality, and inventiveness.

We have witnessed technological advancements that are analogous to the development of radio. Some contend that the era of broadcasting's public value has ended as a result of these advancements. Conversely, the BBC believed that there was a greater necessity than ever for broadcasting to generate public value.

A substantial number of Somalis perceive the BBC Somali services as their property, as they provide the most accurate, reliable, and current information about Somalia.

It was an intriguing phenomenon that the Somali people were so reliant on the transmissions provided by the BBC Somali Service. As soon as the broadcast was scheduled to commence, all individuals would promptly cease their activities and retrieve their radios. A radio programme that lasted for thirty minutes was adequate for engaging in in-depth discourse, despite the time slot being insufficient.

2.4.3: The BBC Contribution to Somali Language

The Somali language experienced explosive growth in the 1980s, and during that time, senior BBC journalists expanded the Somali dictionary by adding newly coined words. (Abdi Yusuf, May 7, 2019) In Somalia, people always actively listen to the radio. To emphasise, the BBC Somali Service was once the production engine for the Somali language, and it used to make significant contributions to the enrichment of the language by adding many new words I created.

The problem is made even worse by the fact that a well-known Somali term, BBC "noo daara" can be translated as "tune BBC radio for us" (ibid). This made it quite evident that the BBC played a significant role in the lives of people, regardless of whether they were looking for content such as news, entertainment, religious education, interviews, or conversations, among other things.

From the perspective of a sizeable portion of Somalis, the BBC was the most trustworthy source of information regarding timekeeping. Quoted by Abdi Yusuf (May 2019), for example, one person can propose, "Let us meet when the afternoon programme concludes" (ibid), while another might claim that their wristwatch is just as accurate as the BBC's. According to Abdi Yusuf (May 2019), historically, Somalis planned their upcoming appointments based on the times when the BBC was broadcasting its various programmes. (ibid.)

The methods and expertise necessary for radio broadcasting differ significantly from those needed for other media forms. Success in radio broadcasting requires a thorough understanding of the fundamental broadcasting language, with particular emphasis on proficiency in speaking and reading the Somali language. The country of origin of the individual who reads or produces the news is irrelevant. The concern pertains to the quality of the news. An individual from Garissa, Kenya, may exhibit greater proficiency in Somali than a person from Somalia.

2.4.4: Relocation of the BBC Somali Service

In 2017, the BBC Somali service underwent a partial relocation to Nairobi, Kenya, where it engaged numerous staff members hailing from the Northeastern region of the country. Nonetheless, owing to complications surrounding work permits, numerous skilled and experienced Somali journalists found themselves unable to pursue employment opportunities with the BBC in Nairobi, a situation largely dictated by the particularities of their passports. This matter merits additional scrutiny. At certain points, the BBC Somali service necessitated the involvement of more specialised individuals,

Part Two
The BBC Somali Language

A notable challenge confronting the BBC Somali service was insufficient editing, with many of these concerns arising from the translation process. It is probable that the majority of news articles featured on BBC Somali are derived from BBC News English. Nevertheless, the act of translation demands a considerable degree of proficiency.

A notable challenge encountered was the recruitment of journalists lacking a foundational understanding of the educational system or international geography.

Abdullahi Haji
My Life Through News Media

Part Three:
Somalia's Media

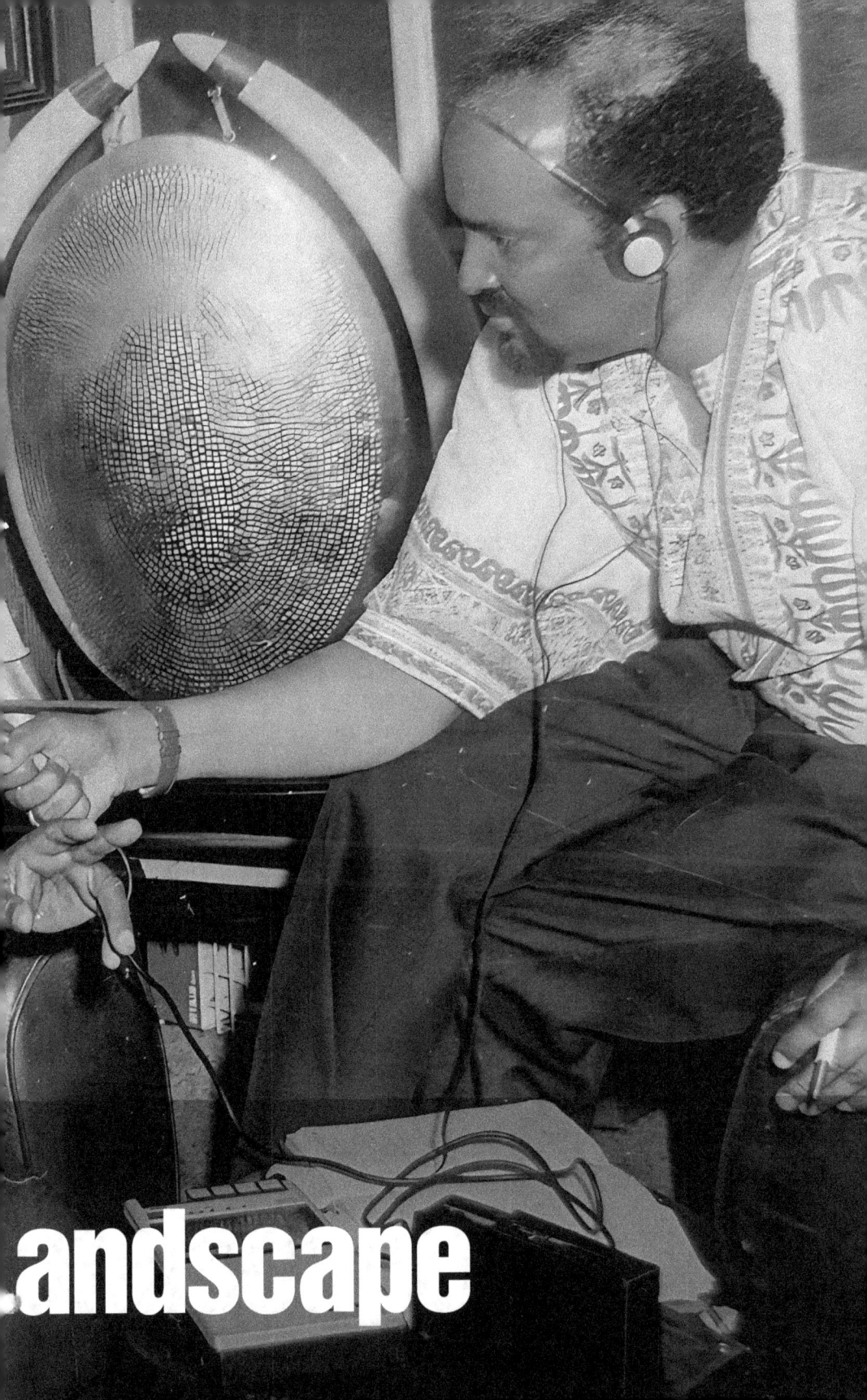

CHAPTER 3

THE IMPACT OF MEDIA ON SOCIETY

In Somalia, the media holds significant importance. It can be posited that Somalia's society is one of the most media-literate on the African continent. In spite of its numerous divisions, a shared linguistic heritage and a profound appreciation for poetry unite this deeply fragmented, war-ravaged nation presently afflicted by drought and famine.

Consequently, there has been an insatiable appetite for news and information in recent history. In this historically pastoralist and nomadic civilisation, the acquisition of information and the

Part Three
Somalia's Media Landscape

assessment of its reliability have consistently shaped not only the political landscape, societal structures, and cultural practices, but also the prospects for survival. Numerous greetings in Somali, such as «maxaad sheegtay,» translate directly to «what news do you have?» They possess the discernment to identify areas to avoid peril and to obtain ample grazing and water sources.

Somali culture embodies a spirit of ambition, self-governance, and a resolute independence from external influences seeking to impose control. This is illustrated by the remarkable courage and sacrifice that define the Somali tradition of news dissemination.

In Somalia, various domains of strife exist, yet the media stands out as one of the most consistent elements. The significance of the matter is underscored by the considerable time and effort expended by those in power to suppress, intimidate, or co-opt the media. The consensus among the individuals surveyed for this briefing indicates that any political resolution within the nation will necessitate public endorsement, thereby emphasising the vital function of the media.

The media serves as a platform for individuals to deliberate on their futures, navigate their conflicts, and, generally speaking, seek resolutions. It provides an essential safeguard against the occasional abuse of power. Throughout its history, Somalia has endured a notably higher incidence of egregious power abuse compared to many other nations. Individuals often misuse and take advantage of the media with remarkable efficacy to exert control, manipulate narratives, and incite conflict, animosity, and discord.

This policy briefing seeks to offer a concise overview of the impact that Somalia's media has had on the nation's historical trajectory, current state, and prospective developments. The findings are grounded in research conducted by the BBC World Service Trust (BBC WST) across the three devastated regions of Somalia.

This briefing adopts an expansive interpretation of media, concentrating primarily on the methods by which Somalis engage with, utilise, trust, and occasionally mismanage information. Various media modalities exert a significant impact on the political and social landscape of Somalia. Nonetheless, radio continues to be the medium that reaches the largest audience and exerts the greatest influence. (Barker et al., 2001)

In Somalia, the introduction of the Latin Somali language alphabet in 1972 coincided with a rich tradition of oral storytelling, establishing radio as a pivotal medium for numerous generations. The primary emphasis of this briefing was on radio access and control; however, it existed alongside other media that are gaining significance.

The economy of the anarchy-capitalist South Central region of Somalia is primarily propelled by a substantial and communication-reliant diaspora, alongside services associated with communications. Somalia's status as having the lowest international call rates in Africa is not merely coincidental. The straightforward accessibility of social media for the populace has replaced the conventional function of radio, owing to the growing prevalence of internet connectivity.

3.1: RADIO: MEDIA & MODERATING FACTOR

Following the collapse of the Somali state, radio transformed into a comparatively centralised medium due to its mode of transmission. Due to bandwidth constraints, a limited number of channels in Somalia were capable of transmission, necessitating a certain level of centralised oversight. Consequently, radio transformed into a medium that facilitated solely one-directional communication. A limited cadre of producers engaged a substantial audience that attentively absorbed radio transmissions on local stations. Considering the attributes of production, distribution, and circulation, it may largely be regarded as a variant of mainstream media.

As previously noted, various factions, including President Siyad Barre, warlords, and Al-Shabab, have sought to exert influence over the media to advance their particular objectives. From an economic

Part Three
SOMALIA'S MEDIA LANDSCAPE

perspective, it appeared that extreme or unilateral media was experiencing diminishing success in Somalia, primarily due to the general lack of support from the populace. The scarcity of extremist content did not inherently indicate a yearning for it, thereby enhancing the moderating role of media, particularly radio, within Somali society.

In Somalia, the radio market generally leans towards moderation—particularly when it operates independently. When warlords seized control of or established a radio station to impose loyalty on behalf of their clan, they encountered a significant challenge. Somalis possess a multifaceted clan structure, characterised by a finite array of principal clans along with numerous minor clans, each governed by its own distinct leader.

In a fragmented political landscape, fostering an audience through content that requires loyalty to a singular political figure is challenging, particularly as Somalis have become more discerning regarding the narratives being presented. When afforded the opportunity and autonomy, Somali audiences exhibit a propensity to engage with a diverse array of perspectives on the radio.

A UNDP employee noted, "It appears that radio stations are often established to advance clan interests, yet they struggle to achieve commercial viability due to a lack of appeal to advertisers." (BBC, November 2011) Without the oppressive influence of Al-Shabab on the media landscape, the imperative of ensuring the financial sustainability of media outlets would dictate their intrinsic allure.

Moreover, financial factors limit Al-Shabab's efforts to sway the media, notwithstanding their brutality. Some authors suggest that individuals have been disengaging from radios operated by Al-Shabab. Consequently, each Friday, they predominantly transmitted sermons from the Al-Shabab leader, accompanied by Quranic material and its translation. Nevertheless, when one probes the attentiveness of individuals, particularly Kismayo, the responses tend to be unfavourable.

Abdullahi Haji
My Life Through News Media

Numerous individuals have indicated that a primary constraint in recent years has been Al-Shabab's prohibition on the dissemination of music and song broadcasts. Instead of receiving perspectives from impartial news sources, individuals are exposed to the narratives of Islamists who are actively recruiting new adherents, seizing governmental control, or enforcing Sharia law. Consequently, individuals residing in regions influenced by Islamist ideologies seek impartial perspectives by discreetly tuning into BBC and VOA. In regions governed by Al-Shabab, broadcasting Quranic recitations on a radio station is a prudent choice.

The station forbids the playing of music as well as any discourse considered disrespectful towards Al-Shabab. Consequently, there is often a significant drop in audience engagement, leading to a di-

IMAGE 8:
From left to right: Asha . the author Abdulahi Haji, and Ambassador Sharif Salah.

minishment of the radio station's political clout. Advertisers tend to withdraw whenever possible, resulting in financial losses alongside a reduction in influence.

The economic climate in Somalia, especially in South Central Somalia, presents significant challenges for the viability of radio stations." According to Daudi Aweis (BBC, November 2011), radio stations in Mogadishu previously garnered advertisements from local businessmen; however, the prevailing instability in the capital has led to a decline in advertising revenue." Fear and aggression have not only wiped out journalism and journalists, but they also threaten stations' ability to connect with their audiences and survive. Research conducted through interviews for this briefing indicated that only a small fraction of station managers engage in the broadcasting of entertainment programmes.

This development is quite predictable, given that in 2010, the Islamist group Hizbul Islam prohibited music, advertisements, and entertainment from private stations in Mogadishu, alongside the existing ban imposed by Al-Shabab. A thorough analysis of the radio show schedules indicated that Radio Hargeisa uniquely offered music and songs in Somaliland, while Radio Xurmo distinguished itself by broadcasting a drama programme weekly on Fridays. (BBC, November 2011) Nonetheless, certain stations persist in transmitting as much as 11 hours of poetry each week. In Somalia, the presence of extremism presents major hurdles for both commercial enterprises and the cultivation of an engaged audience.

3.2: THE ETHIOPIAN – SOMALI WAR

The Ethiopian–Somali Border War of 1964, commonly called the first Ogaden war, marked the first military engagement between the nascent Somali Republic and the Ethiopian Empire. The relationship between Somalia and Ethiopia was marked by a significant border conflict, especially in the Ogaden region, which culminated in the 1964 Ethiopian-Somali border war. During the parliamentary election, Prime Minister Abdirashid Ali Sharmarke articulated a statement asserting that Somalia would engage in voting with one hand while the other hand would be dedicated to the war with Ethiopia. The Ethiopian engaged fully to destroy the newly independent Somali Republic.

The duration extended from February to April of that particular year. The border confrontation was foreshadowed by a significant liberation event occurring in the Ogaden region during the mid-1963 period. This uprising was orchestrated by Somalis advocating for autonomy from colonial dominance. A swift decline in relations between Ethiopia and Somalia ensued due to the subsequent suppression of insurgents and the more severe retaliatory measures implemented by the regime of Emperor Haile Selassie. The rebellion ultimately resulted in a direct confrontation between the military forces of the two nations.

In 1978, following Somalia's defeat in the Ogaden War, the stability of the Siyad administration faced significant challenges, and the nation encountered a rise in clan pressures. The failed military coup of April 1978 set the stage for the emergence of two opposition factions.

The opposition emerged in the wake of the unsuccessful military coup of 1978. Both of these organisations conducted their guerrilla operations from bases in Ethiopia.

Siyad Barre was compelled to improve relations with Kenya and Ethiopia due to these pressures, along with the influence of Western supporters of Somalia. The peace treaty established in 1988 with Ethiopian leader Mengistu Haile Mariam mandated both parties to cease support for Somali antigovernment insurgents, ironically resulting in the subsequent eruption of civil war in Somalia.

During the 1990s, the opposition factions faced the imminent threat of having their bases in Ethiopia shut down, prompting them to initiate offensives against government forces within their territories. Their efforts culminated in a devastating conflict that resulted in the governmental forces asserting dominance over abandoned settlements. The Ogaden liberation movements experienced a gradual integration into the army and militia, leading to a growing sense of disillusionment regarding the peace agreement with Ethiopia. Consequently, the Ogaden liberation movements began to abandon and attack the Somali forces.

As Siyad became progressively fixated on the nuances of daily survival, he adeptly consolidated his control over Mogadishu. Following the emergence of armed oppositions as a paradigm, clan-based guerrilla factions rapidly proliferated and disseminated across the nation.

In January of 1991, military offensives initiated by opposition factions culminated in the ousting of President Siyad Barre. Outside of Mogadishu, all of the major clans that had access to the massive amounts of military weaponry in the country established their own areas of control. The governmental structure in the southern regions had effectively disintegrated, leaving only local governance intact in the northeastern areas.

In May 1991, the Northern Opposition Group declared the 1960 federation null and asserted that the northern territory would henceforth be recognised as an independent entity, designated as the Republic of Somaliland. This proclamation was issued subsequent to the armed northern opposition seizing control of the northern territory that had formerly constituted a segment of British Somaliland.

3.3: UNIFICATION OF SOMALI TERRITORIES

Following the conclusion of World War II, Somali leaders in the Ogaden region of Ethiopia made multiple demands for self-determination, but both Ethiopia and the United Nations chose to dismiss their requests. On July 1, 1960, Italian Somalia achieved its independence and unified with British Somaliland, forming the Somali Republic.

One of the key goals of the Somali Republic was to unify Greater Somalia, which included the Ogaden region. This was one of the primary aims of the Somali Republic. It was one of the most essential objectives that the Somali Republic wanted to accomplish. In the immediate aftermath of the establishment of the Republic of Somalia, the Ethiopian government, recognising the imminent threat posed by Somalis, rapidly dispatched troops to establish military outposts in the Ogaden region.

As a direct consequence of this, hundreds of Somalis, who made up the majority of the territory's population, were forced to flee their homes and were massacred in August of 1960. The Ethiopian forces, who were the only large Ethiopian presence in the region, were not warmly welcomed by the local populace. This was despite the fact that they were the only Ethiopian military present in the region. In the region, it would be another two years before a full-scale rebellion would begin to take place. The Ethiopian government, during this time period, withdrew the grazing rights of a considerable number of Somali nomads, which significantly escalated the conflict.

This particular occurrence occurred during the time period in question. After a series of attacks on nomads that pushed the locals to engage in active self-defense, violent clashes between Ethiopian and Somali military forces began to break out, which finally led to the outbreak of the war in 1964. This fight was the ultimate cause of the war. In the month of April in the year 1961, thousands of Somali refugees made their way to Hargeisa from Dagahbur, which was situated in the Ogaden part of the country. The Ethiopian army had surrounded the city and machine-gunned its populace, which resulted in the deaths of more than one hundred and fifty Somali soldiers, according to the reports that they received.

It was presumed that this behaviour was a form of revenge because local Somali leaders had submitted a petition for self-determination. This petition was presented. Reports indicate that

Somali Defence Minister Ali Ismail Yaqub authorised attacks on Ethiopian territory in the same year.

These raids were carried out in Ethiopia. Numerous Ethiopian bases that were situated along the border were the targets of these raids, which resulted in their destruction. As a result of these battles, around one hundred people from both sides suffered casualties. <Ethiopian authorities taking the place of Somali district commissioners in the Ogaden region heightened concerns about the likelihood of an "Ethiopianization" of the Somali territory. When Ethiopian officials took over, the situation, which was already volatile, became even more violent.

This situation was already potentially explosive. The Somali government would offer help to the Bale insurrection that had begun in 1963 among the Somali and Oromo communities of Ethiopia. This rebellion had been started by the Somali people..

3.4: THE OGADEN LIBERATION FRONT OF 1963

In June of 1963, the Ethiopian government started its first attempts to collect taxes in the Ogaden region. This change was due to the fact that the Somali population had been free from paying taxes for several generations.

The Somali community, which was already unsatisfied with the situation, became bitter as a result of this development. At Hodayo, a watering hole located to the north of Warder, three hundred men chose a former public official to lead an insurgency against the Ethiopians, who are known as "Nasrallah" or the Ogaden Liberation Front. This insurgency was directed against the Ethiopians.

The Western Somali Liberation Front built the foundation that this organisation provides. However, the Somali government did provide some of the liberation movement with the necessary equipment. Despite the fact that the opposition commander, Makhtal Dahir, would later claim that the only significant support that they had received from Somalia was connected to the treatment of wounded and the taking of refugees. This followed the perspective that is held by Somali militants in the Ogaden.

This viewpoint was supplied by Makthal Dahir in a statement that was published in the New York Times describing the beginnings of the insurgency. Twenty-first of July, 1982, New York Times

> "We yearned for our independence. It was impossible to seek democratic rights in a country where there is no freedom of speech and no political party machinery, where expeditions are deployed to collect taxes by force, snatching camels and millet crops, and where there is no political party machinery."

The Emperor vowed to execute 180 Somali leaders in response to their plea for internal self-government. The Ethiopians suspected we were planning something as they were attempting to impose a new head tax on cattle. Additionally, it has been mandated that Quranic schools be closed, and the regulations only allowed one wife and forbade divorce. All of this disrupted Somali Muslim customs. The Ethiopians began arresting people to scare the populace after learning of the opposition's disobedience. However, by that time, the insurgencies had gone into hiding and subsequently formed a liberation movement.

3.4.1: Mass Communication Setting in Somalia

However, the concept of free media is fundamental to democratic regimes, and state media is often associated with dictatorships.

Radio was previously susceptible to political control; however, the concept of free media is essential even today. It is essential, from a political perspective, to maintain a gap between oneself and political control. It is possible for us to achieve this goal by establishing a separate authority that is independent of the state and is responsible for controlling radio. Commercial radio is forced to compete with the BBC, which is an organisation that receives public funding, resulting in a decrease in both its audience and its earnings. Another essential component was the significant influence that was exerted in the realm of cultural politics.

Because of its "difficult" nature and the fact that it did not achieve commercial success, the high culture of BBC Radio 3 maintained a substantial amount of value. The purpose of this was to acquire a more in-depth understanding of the political disagreements that are associated with the functions of the BBC Somali programme..

3.4.2: The Influence of Mass Media

Media influence is the genuine power that is exerted by a media message, which eventually results in either a change or reinforcement of the opinions held by any individual or audience.

The phrase «media influence» refers to the power that is expressed by a media message. McLuhan's work from 1964 states that several factors, including the demographics of the audience and the psychological characteristics of its members, are responsible for determining whether or not a message that is transmitted by the media has an effect on any of its members, whether that influence is positive or negative, abrupt or gradual, short-term or long-lasting. It's possible that these influences will lead to positive or negative outcomes. Some media messages reinforce existing beliefs, but not all consequences lead to a shift.

The audience is investigated by researchers for changes in cognition, belief systems, and attitudes, as well as the emotional, physiological, and behavioural effects induced by media exposure. This occurs when the audience is exposed to media (ibid). The influences of the media, which are frequently referred to as «media effects,» can be observed in a wide variety of aspects of human existence. These aspects include voting behaviours, perceptions of violence, evaluations of scientists, and our ability to comprehend others' perspectives.

There has been a substantial shift in the overall influence of the media over the course of the years, and it is anticipated that this transition will continue as the media itself continues to undergo further development. In the context of new media, our identities as consumers and creators are intertwined. By making use of new media, not only are we able to acquire knowledge, but we are also able to communicate that knowledge to a large number of others. Additionally, there is a major negative impact that the media has on the psychological and social development of children. This impact is quite detrimental.

Thus, doctors must talk to parents about their kids' media exposure and how to use it properly, including TV, radio, music, video games, and the Internet. Investigating the effects of media has been the subject of several studies that have been carried out in academic institutions. As a result of the social, cultural, and psychological consequences that were caused by communicating through the media, they came up with the phrase «media effects.»

According to Marshall McLuhan (1964), they are "… researchers that study media effects [and] investigate how to control, enhance, or mitigate the impact of the mass media on individuals and society." McLuhan also says that they want to know the answer because they want to know what kinds of content, in what kinds of mediums, affect which people, and under what conditions.

Within the framework of his theory of media ecology, McLuhan makes the remark that "the medium is the message for the message." Throughout the course of study on the effects of media, there have been many stages that are collectively referred to as media effects paradigms. In many cases, these phases coincide with the development of technology that is employed in mass media institutions..

3.4.3: The Power of The Impacts Phase of The Media

At the time, it was widely believed that the new technologies of mass communication, such as radio and film, had an almost irresistible power to mould the beliefs, cognition, and behaviours of an audience in line with the desires of the communicators. During the early part of the 20th century, this was the situation.

Eighteenth, one of the key presumptions of the strong media impacts idea was that audiences were unresponsive and consistent in their behaviour. This was one of the fundamental assumptions. On the contrary, this assumption was not established on empirical evidence; rather, it was founded on certain presumptions about the nature of humanity.

There are two key variables that can be linked to this perception of the effects of mass media. To begin, technologies that were used for mass broadcasting were developing a huge audience, even among households that were thought to be typical. It is likely that the audience's perception of any media effects was muddled as a result of the rate at which information was broadcast, which caused them to accumulate.

This is because the audience was exposed to a large amount of information. During the battle, various countries employed propaganda methods as a powerful instrument with the intention of bringing their respective populations together to achieve their goals. These propaganda pieces were superb instances of communication that had a significant impact on audience members.

When the study of the effects of the media was still in its early phases, it typically focused on the influential character of propaganda. Early theories of media effects proposed that the all-powerful nature of the mass media was the result of the confluence of technology and social contexts. These views were based on empirical evidence.

3.5: A BRIEF OVERVIEW OF RADIO HISTORY

The influence of radio on Somalia's politics, culture, and society is greater than that of any other kind of media. On the other hand, other forms of media, both well-established and relatively new, such as the internet and mobile devices, also have considerable influence.

Platforms that are considered traditional media include radio, television, and newspapers. In the majority of the world's poorest countries, radio continues to be the medium that is used most frequently; this is especially true in a nation that has an oral culture that is as firmly rooted as it is. In a statement made by Sahra Abdi, a journalist for Voice of America (VOA) and Reuters News Agency, she says, "Everything that happens in Somalia has a giant impact because everyone listens to the radio and politicians pay attention to what is being said."

Much of this briefing is about radio's role in the media, politics, and society. In spite of the fact that the availability of electricity tends to limit its utilisation to individuals who have a higher level of financial stability, the consumption of electricity is becoming increasingly popular, and political interests are increasingly competing for it.

A 2007 BBC study in Mogadishu found that one-third of participants had watched TV at least once in the past week.

In recent times, not only has the Transitional Federal Government (TFG) in Mogadishu established television stations, but Al-Shabab has also done the same thing. In light of this, it is quite evident that the platform is becoming increasingly important. Mohammed Adow, a journalist for Al Jazeera, explains that the television industry in Somalia is still in its infancy. They have been able to build up their strength over the course of the past three years.

Advertising from London next to those from shops in Mogadishu was seen in demonstration of the efforts that Somali television was making to bridge the divide between people who live outside the nation and those who live within it. A scenario in which satellite television transmission emerged as the most influential form of media would not surprise me in the least.

Part Three
Somalia's Media Landscape

IMAGE 19:
*The author Abdulahi Haji reporting from Buckingham Palace in London 1981.
Courtesy of Farhan Jimale @farhanjimale https://x.com/farhanjimale*

In addition to the fact that this is a relatively new industry, there is an explosion of satellite television platforms. According to a BBC report from November 2011, the majority of these satellite television platforms are located outside of Somalia, with Universal TV being the most well-known institution based in London.

Television stations can broadcast Somali songs and dances that are accessible, with the exception of regions that are controlled by Al-Shabab. This has resulted in Somalia having one of the most developed online media landscapes in Africa. In recent years, Somalia has witnessed a growth of internet sites, notably social media news sites.

This expansion has led to the country having its own unique online media environment. Somalia is distinguished by the vastness of its diversity and the usually turbulent nature of its environment. People often have various opinions when it comes to this continually changing scene, which is similar to how the media represents itself.

The substantial Somali diaspora has been responsible for the formation of a considerable chunk of the country. Over three million Somalis currently reside outside of Somalia, which has resulted in the internet media gaining a large amount of authority within the country.

3.5.1: Supporting the Somali Media Sector

Somalia is largely acknowledged by the international community as one of the most dangerous places for journalists to work. The region is currently experiencing anarchy, a lack of resources and infrastructure, and political instability as a result of a protracted period of war.

The region's situation has been made worse by a terrible famine that has lately occurred. In order for Somalis to communicate directly with local authorities, express their ideas, and participate in public discourse, the media is crucial in helping them obtain

Part Three
SOMALIA'S MEDIA LANDSCAPE

and use information. It is essential to comprehend and support the media sector since it helps to address some of the problems facing the country. As part of a media development project, BBC Media Action carried out a thorough investigation into the role and status of the media in Somali society between 2010 and 2012.

Additionally, the project trained Somali civil society organisations in communication, especially those that advocate for women and youth. The project also provided management staff, senior editors, and journalists with training at radio stations. (BBC, November 2011)

3.5.2: The Danger Zone

It is undeniably difficult for journalists to operate in Somalia. There is a pervasive tendency for people to self-censor, and competing political pressures threaten the production of objective news. Organisations monitoring press freedom record a startlingly high number of cases of journalist harassment, attacks and killings, asset seizures, and even radio station closures.

In spite of this, there are a sizable number of media outlets operating in every Somali region, and journalists are generally considered having a high standing among the general public. The results of the study show that audiences have a strong thirst for news and development-focused content. Diana Njeru, the project coordinator, pointed out that there is a lot of work in this category::

> "We train journalists to share information that offers hope at the end of a dark journey," she explained to reporters. The journalists with whom I collaborate are courageous individuals. They aspire for the world to hear the stories of Somalia." (Diana Njeru, 2025)

3.5.3: Various News Sources

In Somalia, radio remains the most powerful media outlet. Because of the crumbling infrastructure brought on by years of strife, newspapers are almost nonexistent in some areas, especially those outside of large capitals. The growing significance of television is evidenced by the recent establishment of television stations by the federal administration and the Islamist rebel group Al-Shabab.

Nonetheless, television availability is still limited across the nation. More people are using mobile phones and other new forms of communication, especially for face-to-face interactions. Despite being mainly untapped, it has the potential to improve communication and information goals.

3.6: PERSON WHO PROMOTES MODERATION?

A policy briefing by BBC Media Action, which was based on the research findings, indicates a cautious optimism despite the apparent terrible situation. Some argue that Somalia's media may have a moderating influence. According to the briefing, numerous clan leaders have tried to use the radio to further their own personal agendas in the past, which has led to conflict, mistrust, and stress.

On the other hand, the world might benefit from the media as well. Sponsored media has been asserted to help improve regional stability in response to the demand of common Somalis for trustworthy and useful information.

Njeru (2025) states that «Somalis may feel forgotten and ignored, but that doesn't mean they have given up hope.» «Somalia has been ruled by chaos for far too long, but people are starting to imagine a better future," she says.

3.6.1: The Future Prospect of Somali Social Media

Prospects for the upcoming years: Almost all of the study's interviewees concurred that funding journalist training and capacity building is crucial. Two of the main problems Somalists faced were intimidation and incapacity, and they were intimately related to each other. In the last ten years or so, a considerable number of professional journalists have left the country, and since 2007, they have been leaving every day.

A member of the National Union of Somali Journalists (NUSOJ), Ahmednur Mohamed Farah, claims that most of the journalists currently employed in Southern Somalia are new employees who have just entered the field. They are trainees in large numbers. Most journalists now working in Somalia have less than five years of field experience, according to research conducted for the BBC World Service.

This trend has not only cost the nation many accomplished journalists, but it has also led to a shortage of skilled mentors who can teach aspiring journalists the values and techniques of journalism.

Research involving both media experts and viewers indicates that both groups think that journalism has become less good recently. They failed to incorporate different points of view into their examples and instead provided examples of biased and inaccurate output. Both the ability and the record to carry out investigative journalism seem to have significantly decreased. A wide range of skills, such as basic journalism abilities, objectivity, an understanding of particular topics (including governance, gender, and refugees), and professional and business management skills, are said to require training.

However, a large number of Somali journalists and other people continue to challenge the principles that define media. The aforementioned journalists lack adequate experience in the journalism industry. The media outlets have never provided any fresh information to most of them.

They must study the ethics of journalism. Sahra Abdi asserts that "if you do not know the ethics of journalism, it will cause harm, even to yourself." Somalia's government went from repressive to lawless in 1991. Omar Qadi says this event has made the media one of the world's most chaotic.

Journalist for Al Jazeera One journalist has stated that there is insufficient training. Ahmednur Mohamed Farah claims that:

> "Not only do you need to provide the journalists with fundamental training on how to be objective, but you also need to provide them with training that teaches them how the global media operates. I believe there should be more training for journalists, particularly training on human rights, good governance, impartiality, and advocacy. Some media owners don't know media law, and some journalists don't know journalism ethics, so journalists must learn their rights". (Ahmednur Mohamed Farah, 2015)

He adds that there is still a serious problem with equipment shortages. This assertion is corroborated by research from the BBC World Service Team, which revealed significant issues with vital broadcasting equipment, generator capacity, internet connectivity, and audio recording facilities.

3.6.2: What Factors Increased Somali Media Such as Websites?

The Somali civil conflict has progressed into a new phase since the late 1990s: the media war. The website evolved into a tool for advancing collective political identity. Similar to personal webpages, these websites function as venues for self- or group presentation. An identity crisis occurs when a society starts to fall apart during a time of social or economic upheaval. By expressing and associating with alternative discourses, people attempt to reconstruct their identities and social significance in such circumstances.

Every community has tried to recover its identity as a result of the state «virus» being rolled back. Such a place is provided on the

Part Three
SOMALIA'S MEDIA LANDSCAPE

webpage. The number of Somali websites was less than twenty in 1998. As this study developed, a large number of websites were classified.

There are two main reasons for the growth of Somali websites:
1) The loss of national identity as a result of the breakdown of governmental institutions, and
2) The conversational characteristics of the Internet, which are expressive, interactive, and engagement-based.

The first reason is influenced by the new political and social environment that developed following the state's dissolution, which led people to reestablish ties to their ancestors. Because of its fundamental architecture, which is distinguished by a conspicuous lack of central authority, the Internet could be regarded as a somewhat democratic technology.

A further explanation for the proliferation of Somali websites and the development of communication technologies, including telecommunications, may be found in this parallel, since the disorderly nature of Somali websites can be seen as a feature of ‹pastoral democracy.›

There are several factors that contribute to the growth of Somali websites, including:
a) The domestic political elite who have taken advantage of this new communication channel;
b) The educated Somalis who have had the chance to interact with and use the CMC medium; and
c) The Diaspora's long-lasting influence on local Somali politics, which has been present since the 1940s, when Somali nationalism first emerged..

In the early 1990s, attempts were made in several parts of Europe and North America to create locally oriented newspapers based on clan ties. However, very few continued over the first year or the first four payments. Kasmo is a notable exception among Somali newspapers, having been founded on September 27, 1997. It is a daily known for its independence and nonpartisan position, was founded. Its continued existence depends on its work being shared with a wider audience and the patience of its editors, Abduqadir Shire and Khalid Macow.

Khalid Mao had previously been a university lecturer, while Abdulqadir Shire was editor of Heegan, the Somali Revolutionary Party's publication. In 2004, smo started publishing its East Africa Kasmo edition, which is distributed across the Middle East and East Africa, including Somalia.

With a dedicatioSince its founding in 1998, Kasmo has maintained impartiality and independence by publishing in London. lities of print, which demand an efficient distribution mechanism, highlight the fact that the field of web design has surpassed traditional printing. An electronic newspaper can save money and time when it comes to publishing, updating, and storing information.

AdditionallyAdditionally, there are lower expenses and less time required for creating and editing electronic material. to lowering manufacturing costs, electronic storage and retrieval also reduces the amount of space needed for document storage. This lowers costs even more. Furthermore, sharing content online automatically exposes it to a global audience. Web pages, as opposed to printed products, contain a wide range of components, including visual images, audio, and text. In comparison to print media, web pages are more dynamic and easily editable. The process of creating websites reflects the development of identities, exposing the complex interrelationships between the makers and their own perceptions of themselves. According to Issa-Salwe (1991), web pages offer a special venue for self- or group presentation.

3.7: MANAGING INFORMATION

According to Issa-Salwe (2008), running news online, for example, necessitates information management, which Somali radio news must confront often. Managing such things necessitates additional abilities such as prioritising news, recognising news values, and news selection. A notable element of this circumstance is the development of new skills by Somali webmasters. They must use their skills as propaganda while maintaining journalistic standards.

Since the year 2000, the Internet with social media has served as the primary source of home news for the Somalis. For example, since 2000, the BBC has offered an Internet version of Somali news. Users can download and listen to BBC programmes at their leisure via the Internet. (Issa-Salwe, 2008)

Prior to the year 2000, much web content contained low-quality material. Recently, professional online journalism skills have become essential for operating such services due to competition and the need to adapt to a changing environment, as well as technological advancements. Somali newsmakers face the difficult duty of providing their viewers with the best selection of news articles. Because news is chosen, it is frequently asserted that it has an «agenda-setting» function, with the themes in the news forming an explicit political agenda. Chandler (1997) argues that news items are actively manufactured, rather than merely selected.

Newsmakers are also required to possess the ability to attract and persuade their target audience. Because of the impact of the civil war and mistrust, the Somali audience is more likely to trust and believe what is published on their «own» group's radio or websites.

One viewpoint expresses, «Although the information published by other websites may be accurate, I do not feel compelled to trust it.» (Issa-Salwe, 2008). At the same time, people have access to considerably more information, empowering them to make their own news decisions.

Regardless, the user is not at the stage where the online journalist chooses or selects content. Online journalism, as an Internet-based communication, requires a distinct media logic that differs from that of print and broadcast media (Dahlgren 1996). Online journalism is one instance where the question of how this media logic is generated emerges. It is stated as gathering and distributing news material only via the Internet, and it is conceptualised here as "a fourth kind of journalism next to print, radio, and television journalism with its own specific journalistic characteristic" (Deuze, 2001).

Because news is the primary component of newspapers, it is challenging to convey it without referencing the medium (the website) itself. Some consider news to be a reflection of social settings, whereas others, such as Walter Lippman (1992), define it as «not a mirror of social conditions, but the report of an aspect that has obtruded itself" (ibid). In this way, attention is drawn to what is unique and worthy of notice in a structure appropriate for planned and routine inclusion in a news report (McQuail, 1994: 268).

> Another early news commentator, Robert Park (1940), concentrated on the key aspects of the news report. His starting point was to compare it to other "categories of knowledge," such as history, and place news on a scale ranging from "acquaintance with" to "knowledge about" (Park, 1940)..

News is somewhere in the middle of the range (ibid.). Park's investigation revealed that news events are distinguished by numerous ‹news values,' which are always relative and involve subjective judgements of expected audience interest (ibid. 45). Sociocultural factors appear to play a significant role in the selection of community/political news types. In this aspect, news values tend to highlight events involving war and conflict. Websites typically prioritise news events that they believe will satisfy both their audience and their needs. (Issa-Salwe, 2008)

Although judgements of news importance are frequently relative and dependent on a journalist's «feel for news» at the time, there are usually significant aspects of subjectivity.. The news code's norms are more likely to be shown in how events are handled and reported than in their selection or neutrality.

Hubsiino hal baa la siistaa (Certainty worth a she-camel).

Conversely, the following aphorism demonstrates the nomads' intolerance to uncertainty: Kugu dishaa waged war on la Faani. Wehel la'aanna wadadaa kugu dheeraata. Waddan aqoon la'aanna waabashaa kuku disha. (A lack of news causes fear). Loneliness makes the journey longer. (Being unfamiliar with the land makes you wary.) (Issa-Salwe, 2008)

The speed and immediacy of the medium, along with the ‹immediately rectifiable› archive capacity of any website, creates a situation in which a journalist may be tempted to sacrifice ethics in favour of a deadline or scoop (ibid.). This fundamentally challenges the need for accuracy (a longstanding professional value in journalism) and pushes journalists to adopt some form of norm. The more accurate online journalism, the better it is. Information is checked in several ways. The Internet enables errors to be corrected promptly, even replacing specific pieces of news information in real' time (Deuze et al., 2001).

Traditionally, Somalis differentiated news bearers into two categories: goob-jooge, who witnessed an incident and is also ‹qualified› to speak authoritatively about what happened, and maqle, who heard the news. Both are evaluated based on the timeliness of the information sources.

> Weris, the first-hand observer's account, is identified as the first, while tebis, the second-hand (or third, fourth, etc.) relationship to the original version, is acknowledged as the second (Academy for Peace and Development, 2002: 13).

Somali webmasters consider information as a commodity, which reflects the Somali culture.

As stated elsewhere, information is considered a vital resource in this culture. ‹*Warbaa ugu gaaja wayn'* (information hunger is the worst hunger), according to Somalis. The Somali culture requires anyone who deals with information to possess the virtue of 'wargalnimo' (literally, information handlers). Accuracy is critical in the news industry, and because websites lack the means to run a news agency (such as paying its reporters), there are always issues with maintaining it. (Issa-Salwe, 2008) Competition, in addition to a shortage of resources, puts strain on the situation.

Wargalnimo is linked to duty in Somali tradition. One of the traits of man is wargalnimo. A man who is incapable of ‹managing information' is considered dishonoured, loses dignity, and so falls into the category of «he whose daughter would not be married» (gabadhaa guurwaa). However, such conventions have deteriorated in recent years, and news readers are less likely to highlight such distinctions, allowing rumours and hearsay to spread more easily. In general, four elements (connected in a different order) can be found in theories of the news-making process: News categories include events, criteria, reports, and topics of interest.

This sequence begins with the phrase ‹obtrude' and breaks the normality, to which the media responds by applying standards of relative relevance for their audience (McQuail, 1994: 136). This approach emphasises the reality-responsiveness of the news, the theoretical perspective, and the structured and autistic nature of the news selection process. They prepare objective news reports about chosen occurrences, and the audience responds with attention and interest or not, which informs subsequent selection behaviour (ibid. 106)..

The alternative sequence is as follows:
news interest, news criteria, events, and news reporting

Part Three
SOMALIA'S MEDIA LANDSCAPE

Here, the beginning point is experience with what catches the public's attention, which contributes to a rather constant and enduring set of news criteria, including organisational and genre requirements. News events are only considered newsworthy if they meet the following selection criteria. News requirements and routeing techniques are determined more by reference to the 'real world' of events or what the audience 'really' wants to read (McQuail, 1994: 274). Websites appear to prefer the last model since it is more attention-grabbing. This inclination may cause the media to cater to the demands and interests of its audience.

The political aspect in online material has a different significance. Audience pleasure is highly valued, and in certain circumstances, it appears that the audience is pleased with what they receive from their preferred website. Here is a mix of satisfaction and political content that prioritises the event. Satisfaction, political substance, and events The importance of an event is determined by the audience's attention (satisfaction). A journalist believes that «considering news events that the audience finds of interest is a first priority» (Issa-Salwe, 2008). In other words, what makes anything appealing appears to be political qualities, which are also greatly sought after by the audience. (Issa-Salwe, 2008).

Abdullahi Haji
My Life Through News Media

Part Four:
Managing Infor

Part Three
SOMALIA'S MEDIA LANDSCAPE

3.8:

CHAPTER 4

ORAL CULTURE AND COMPUTER-MEDIATED COMMUNICATION

THE ENORMOUS BI-DIRECTIONALITY OF THE COMMUNICATION VECTORS ON THE INTERNET IS ARGUABLY ONE OF ITS MOST SIGNIFICANT FEATURES. THE INTERNET CAN FACILITATE INSTANTANEOUS EXCHANGES, WHEREAS TELEVISION AND RADIO ONLY ALLOW INFORMATION TO TRAVEL IN ONE DIRECTION.

The enormous bi-directionality of the communication vectors on the Internet is arguably one of its most significant features. The Internet can facilitate instantaneous exchanges, whereas television and radio only allow information to travel in one direction.

CMC creates a world built on text, exhibiting the traits of a primary oral culture. These technologies change society and thought by establishing communities where people may engage in expressive, emotional, and engaging communication (December, 1993). Orality and literacy can coexist in a forum created by CMC features. For Somalis, oral communication is more enticing because of these features.

According to Issa-Salwe (2008), people could voice their opinions and engage in synchronous discussions. The author compared a face-to-face group with a CMC communication group and discovered that the CMC group generated more ideas and took longer to reach a decision. Additionally, more emotions were expressed, and involvement was more equitable. He argues that orality and literacy exist along a continuum. The oral approach develops from the emphasis on interpersonal interaction between the speaker/writer and the listener, depending on how much the communicator concentrates on involvement or message substance (ibid).

4.8.1: The Internet and Oral Qualities

In the Issa-Salwe (1996) analysis, McLuhan expressed that the lack of "aural space" is the reason why writing has never been a major form of communication in Somali society. McLuhan claimed that the involvement, expression, and participation of the world of primary orality were destroyed by print culture. The print world was to be founded on linear thought, abstraction, and the division of the knower from the known, rather than a world of sound and involvement (December, 1993). Somalis may have developed an extremely rich oral culture as a result of their need to protect their "aural space." (ibid.)

According to John December (1993), there is an emerging «discourse culture» on the Internet that exhibits characteristics of oral communication while yet being textual. His theory makes use of Walter Ong's descriptions of the characteristics of groups that are going through a «primary orality.» (Ong, 1982)

Ong (1982) proposed that although there will be some differences, some aspects of orality are anticipated to reappear in an electronic culture. Tannen's thesis that oral methods develop from an emphasis on interpersonal participation between speaker/writer and audience—which depends on social context and shared interpersonal context for meaning—is the foundation for December's explanation of orality (December, 1994). By using Tanner's theory, Ong was able to identify oral features in Internet users' textual comments, which are recognised for having a recognisable style and a personal tone. He contends that Ong's eight "primary" traits of oral communication and cognition can be effectively "applied to" or "seen within" the many forms of net.text interaction that are frequently encountered on the Internet (ibid.).

Somali online forums and website content also exhibit some of the traits of «primary» oral communication and cognition. An Internet forum, or the web application software that provides the feature, is a platform for hosting discussions on the World Wide Web that functions similarly to newsgroups. Forums that have a high level of user engagement are likely to cultivate a strong sense of virtual community.

The oral properties of the Internet shall be examined below using samples of different Somali forum extracts as case studies. Among these characteristics are conservative or traditionalist, redundant or «copious,» and additive or aggregative..

4.8.2: Tendencies In Oral

The inclination to add or aggregate is one of CMC's oral traits. Instead of using subordinate clauses, this inclination is to merely employ additive primary clauses. Parataxis is frequently used in additive oral speech patterns to show the links between clauses

(Ong, 1982). Clauses that end in "and" serve as examples of this additive property.

4.8.3: Where Should We Go From Here?

Three issues have garnered widespread recognition and repeated attention:

a) Media freedom protection (particularly in relation to the provision of more effective assistance to journalist unions and associations);
b) Journalist training and capacity building; and
c) Policy and regulation enhancement. Nevertheless, certain research concepts could serve as the foundation for such a strategy.

The following principles have emerged, despite the fact that the purpose of this policy briefing is not to establish a strategy for assisting Somali media: Establish the media's assistance as a top priority. Within the context of a society that is in dire need of moderation, this briefing makes the argument that the media has the capacity to be a profoundly moderating force.

We should consider an urgent, coordinated, and long-term programme of support for the media sector in Somalia that is essential to establishing a durable political settlement in the nation. This is despite the fact that the media sector in Somalia faces various obstacles, such as its complexities, shortcomings, and substantial obstacles. The future media sector in Somalia will be established by Somalis, who will have both ownership and agency.

The legitimacy of initiatives to assist the media of the nation will become increasingly significant. A long-term media support programme is necessary to earn the respect of Somali society, given the country's fragmented nature. One approach to achieving this objective, as per the research findings, is to prioritise the development of existing media's capabilities and strengths through collaboration.

An additional critical component is the provision of training to individual journalists for brief periods. Individuals who are capable of establishing standards and teaching others should be the primary focus of training. We focused on radio station administrators and media editors because they are more likely to be employed by organisations for an extended period than individual journalists. Those media organisations that are the most in need of assistance may receive the most beneficial support.

In the past few years, the primary focus of available support has been on organisations that are simple to work with and typically have fairly high standards. Not only should individuals with exceptional journalistic skills provide instruction, but they should also prioritise the cultivation of new skills and the ethical standards of journalism..

4.8.4: Advocate for Regulatory Reform.

Without functioning institutions, reforming Somalia's regulations is more difficult than in nearly any other country. This is especially true in South Central Somalia. Both national and international organisations have been heavily involved in the heated regulatory disputes. Disagreement has been a common topic in recent years about the level of determination of different administrations to support or censor the media.

This is illustrated, for instance, by the framework within which Islamic media should be promoted. Support for media liberalisation and protection of media freedom varies between authorities, both historically and geographically. But people who are prone to this or who are dealing with pent-up demand for radio licences have the same problem: how to guarantee a free, professional, and diversified media without fostering or, as some may say, re-establishing circumstances that promote additional violence.

A major challenge for the future will be maintaining and strategically bolstering regulatory laws and processes that can resolve this tension. However, if authorities can be sure that liberalising media won't lead to more conflict, they may be more willing to do so. The primary goal of this assistance should be to guarantee that people may access credible and diverse viewpoints from national and international actors.

4.8.5: Information Is High Demand Among the General Public.

Ensuring strategic consistency is essential, considering that the support network for Somali media ranks among the most complex in the world. Strategic coherence holds significance for various reasons, such as the intricate nature of the media landscape, the multitude of domestic media support organisations, the presence of numerous foreign media support entities (including the publishers of this briefing), and the array of external donor organisations.

4.8.6: From Mass Media to Social Media

I have firsthand knowledge of how social media has replaced traditional media. For many people, using social media sites like Facebook and Instagram has become ingrained in their daily lives. Given that the majority of users of these platforms are teenagers and young adults, particularly young women, it is important to consider whether or not using social media affects one's body image, self-esteem, self-concept, and body dissatisfaction.

Researchers have started looking into these issues empirically, and recent research has produced a range of results. This research attempts to analyse the data and offers possible hypotheses for how social media use affects body dissatisfaction. Instagram, Facebook, and other well-known image-based platforms receive special attention..

4.8.7: Influence Exerted by the Media

The utilisation of social media has markedly escalated over the previous decade and continues to progress at a consistent pace. A higher proportion of female teenagers use image-based social media platforms compared to their male counterparts. Research indicates an association between women's exposure to fashion media and the emergence of eating disorders and body dissatisfaction.

This research examined the correlation between media exposure and body image, revealing a potential link between personal body dissatisfaction and the consumption of pictures depicting slender physiques.

Direct mass media exposure pertains to individual media engagement, whereas indirect mass media exposure relates to media engagement experienced by individuals within one's social circle. The study's findings indicate that social networks significantly influence the connection between media and eating disease, potentially extending to a link between media and body dissatisfaction.

This is notwithstanding the study's limitations, including the issue of the generalizability of the findings. These findings, however, must be approached with caution, as other researchers have shown no correlation between the consumption of image-based media and unhappiness with one's physique.

A greater, albeit minimal, prevalence of body dissatisfaction was observed in females, especially among those predisposed to body image issues. Initially, there was a minimal correlation between media exposure and body dissatisfaction in guys. Owing to exaggerated effect sizes, constraints in study design, and publication bias, the meta-analysis generally advised researchers to adopt a more cautious stance on the correlation between social media and body dissatisfaction. Additional factors that influenced this finding encompassed publication bias.

4.8.8: Making Use of Social Media

Social media creates a common space for people to connect with one another, and the number of people who can communicate with each other is practically endless. Many benefits have been identified in relation to the regular use of social media platforms:
1) Enhanced engagements with individuals,
2) Increased accessibility to shared and customised information.
3) Enhanced accessibility and broadened access to health information,
4) Support from peers, social networks, and emotional connections,
5) The monitoring of public health, and
6) Capacity to shape health policy

In their investigation, the researchers discovered these advantages. However, although there are a lot of benefits associated with the utilisation of social media, particularly social media platforms that are based on photographs, there are also some applications of these platforms that may result in consequences that are not acceptable. It is possible for the media to exert a significant amount of influence on young people because of the widespread usage of media, particularly social media, within this age group.

The findings that have been discussed above have started important talks regarding ways in which the use of social media may promote body dissatisfaction. TThese conversations, in turn, provide a basis for future research. Important conversations have been sparked as a result of the findings that have been discussed above.

On the other hand, the bulk of research makes use of correlation methodologies, and the causal mechanisms that are thought to be the basis for the putative relationships are not yet completely known.

In contrast to being relevant to the general population, a sizeable fraction of the findings can be applied to a particular person within the population. In the future, there is a substantial amount of work that has to be done to deconstruct the causes of causation.

Some examples of these causes are the pressure from peers and the capabilities of photo editing software. The need to clarify the construct that is being measured (i.e., whether the result is eating disorder pathology, body dissatisfaction, and so on) is one of these areas.

Another area that needs to be addressed is the necessity to design the whole experiment by addressing the constraints of past research. Past study appears to indicate that there is a connection between social media and body dissatisfaction, although past studies have produced contradictory findings and contain problems. This is despite the fact that the exact nature and degree of the association between social media and body dissatisfaction are still unknown.

4.1: THE MILITARY TAKEOVER OF THE SOMALI BROADCASTING

An military dictatorship that ruled Somalia for twenty-one years may be the source of popular demands for well-established participatory democracy. This desire may be traced back to the moment when Somalia was under its jurisdiction.

When this article was being written, a substantial number of people believed that the requirement of having freedom of thought, speech, and action ought to be weighed against the necessity of maintaining political stability and social harmony.

This theory was held by a significant number of people. This was because the peace was still in a precarious state, and the war was still quite recent in people's memories. In the Somali regions, local administrations, sometimes warlords, are responsible for publishing newspapers. Since 1998, the government of Somaliland has exerted a tremendous level of control over the media in the country. As a consequence, a very large number of individuals have experienced a great deal of anxiety as a result of this control.

Part Three
Somalia's Media Landscape

Puntland's media control is very different from Somaliland's. This is a significant distinction between the two countries. The media in Mogadishu has developed to an incredible degree in comparison to the other parts of Somalia, particularly Somaliland and Puntland, where there has been a relative peace and stability for several years.

In particular, Puntland and Somaliland have been experiencing relative peace and stability. Puntland is a place where this is especially true. This phenomenon happened during the preceding decade, which followed the dissolution of the institutions that had been providing support to the Somali state. It was a consequence of the disintegration of those institutions.

In addition to more than a dozen high-quality newspapers, Mogadishu is home to twelve local shortwave radio stations, two international radio networks, two television stations, and two satellite television stations. Additionally, there are two television stations that are located within the city. As an additional point of interest, there are twelve radio stations located in the vicinity. The city's status as the capital of Somalia and its ability to attract international attention may have been early factors that influenced its development.

A number of variables, including this one, could have contributed to the development. The inability of the metropolis to be managed and the turmoil that can be seen across the city are two more issues that could be taken into consideration.

Consequently, because of the collapse of the state, the city has been split up into competing organisations that are currently competing with one another for control of the nation. At this moment, these organisations are competing with one another over the authority of the nation. It was necessary for each function to develop its own media in order to "fight" against the other functions that were competing with them. A state of "absolute" media freedom has been developed as a result of the subsequent anarchy, which can be referred to as "media anarchy." This atmosphere has been cultivated because of the ongoing anarchy."

4.1.1: My Trip to Addis Ababa

My departure from my apartment in Shepherd's Bush at 5:30 in the morning on October 1st, 1992, marked the beginning of my duty tour to Ethiopia. The first of many difficulties I would face appeared before me almost immediately. The door to my apartment was left unlocked because I was in such a hurry to arrive to Heathrow Airport by six in the morning. Although I had actually closed the front door of the house, I had left the door that led to my apartment wide open. My neighbours, who believed it had been broken into, reported the incident to the authorities. In turn, the police called Florence Akst, who was responsible for the Somali service, to inform her of what had occurred and to let her know that, thankfully, the contents of the flat were not damaged and that nothing appeared to have been taken.

Three and a half hours after landing at Heathrow, we landed at Frankfurt International Airport, where I was waiting to board the Lufthansa flight that was scheduled to take me to Addis Ababa. Our departure from Frankfurt occurred at approximately noon on the first of October, and we arrived in Addis at 1800 hours GMT. Along the way, we stopped at Jeddah's wonderfully sophisticated airport for one hour.

Regrettably, transit passengers were not permitted to disembark from the plane. The break would have provided them with fresh air and a chance to stretch their legs.

This would have let them stretch and breathe fresh air during the break.

Therefore, the exceptionally efficient German crew compensated for any discomfort we might have experienced aboard the contemporary Airbus by providing us with a magnificent meal and taking excellent care of us.

Part Three
Somalia's Media Landscape

The Bole International Airport in Addis Ababa is one of the most cutting-edge airports in all of Africa. However, I found it to be one of the least efficient airports I have ever encountered. There were well over one hundred people coming on the Lufthansa flight, but there were only two immigration agents available to handle them. One of them was a man, and the other was a woman. Over three hours were required for us to pass through the immigration and customs procedure.

Their luggage was subjected to a thorough inspection and search, and they were very stringent. When it was my turn, the customs officer asked me to open my suitcase. Once I did, he immediately started taking everything out of the table and placing it on an old table that had turned grey as a result of its frequent use. I informed him that I would tell him if I had the item he was searching for, but only if he asked me directly about it. I was extremely upset by the whole situation.

When I asked him what he was looking for, he gave me an angry look and stated, «I am looking for contraband items, which you would not tell me if you ever had them.» After further investigation, I discovered that they typically look for large numbers of United States dollars, but they do not look for other items like gold bars, traveller's checks, or illegal substances. I was utterly worn out and fatigued when I got to the Ghion Hotel, which was less than a minute past midnight. I went out for a brief stroll the following morning, which was the second of October, after having a very substantial breakfast consisting of eggs, several slices of toast, jam, and tea.

My goal was to gain an understanding of what life is like in Addis Ababa, as I had been away for more than twenty-seven years and had no prior experience there. Since the armies of Ethiopia's Peoples Revolutionary Democratic Front (EPRDF) overthrew the cruel Marxist rule of Colonel Mengistu Haile Mariam, it has been one and a half years since the regime was overthrown. Col. Mengistu ruled with tyranny for fourteen years, during which time he was responsible for the deaths of hundreds of thousands of people as a result of the wars and famines that he intentionally caused.

I was taken aback by the sheer number of people who were begging; the majority of them were persons with disabilities and young women who were carrying children on their backs. I asked why there were so many beggars on the streets, and the answer I received was that the fabric of society in both rural and urban areas of the country had been completely destroyed as a result of 18 years of unnecessary civil war and a Marxist dogma that had been imposed on the people by Col. Mengistu and his ruthless clique.

A large number of people who had fled the rural areas had gathered in the capital city in the hopes of finding food and a place to live.

As a result of Mengistu's steadfast dedication to his battle, a significant number of these individuals began to perish from malnutrition and illness. The EPRDF government's decision to demobilise more than two hundred thousand former troops made the situation even more dire.

To survive, they frequently resorted to means such as begging, occasionally robbing, and even killing innocent people. It is impossible to accurately estimate the number of people who are begging in Addis Ababa; nonetheless, several individuals, including two drivers, have informed me that they believe there are at least one hundred thousand of them. It was stated by one of them that Addis had turned into a "city of beggars."

When Colonel Mengistu ousted the Revolutionary Council, which was led by General Teferre Benti, in 1977, he immediately established a Marxist-Leninist administration.

The administration's primary professed goal was to improve the quality of life for the people. He came to the conclusion that the most effective method of attaining this objective would be to nationalise all private property, which would include buildings, factories, farms, schools, and so on.

On the other hand, the action had the opposite impact. Although the nationalisation, which was not properly planned, resulted in a substantial reduction in the amount of wealth that was held by private individuals, this did not result in even the tiniest improvement in the living conditions of the urban poor or the rural peasantry. Because of the actions taken by the government, the majority of people were compelled to gather in the capital to flee the civil conflict and the starvation.

After being away from Addis Ababa for 27 years, I observed that the only substantial change was the planting of a large number of trees. These trees had contributed to the enhancement of the city's aesthetic appeal and helped conceal the enormous poverty that had been passed down from the Mengistu era.

A significant number of the city's structures are in dire need of repairs, and the city itself is in a condition of decay. Those who reside in Addis have facial expressions that are a direct result of the depressing atmosphere in which they are immersed.

Although I did not attend any nightclubs or soccer matches, I did not observe a lot of people happy or laughing about anything. Ethiopians are, by their own nature, people who tend to keep to themselves.

On the other hand, it is possible to perceive or experience the profound depression that a nation is experiencing, and the inhabitants of Addis Ababa appeared to me as if they were rising from a terrifying nightmare.

The photo made me think: if the EPRDF, a relatively free and democratic government, has such low morale, how bad would it have been under Colonel Mengistu, who is known for his cruelty? It has to have been a terrible experience. Although there is food available, I observed several severe cases of malnutrition, notably among mothers who were caring for youngsters.

At one point, while I was making my way up the «Churchill Road» that leads to the «Piazza,» which is the central business district of the city, I noticed a young man standing on the side of the road.

Holding his knees firmly in his hands and bearing a big stone on his shoulders, he was hunched over to the point of being unrecognisable. He took a piece of grey cloth that was soiled with filth and laid it out in front of him. To find out why he was putting such a strain on himself, I approached him and asked him. The response he gave me jolted me a little bit. According to him, the people have lost their capacity for compassion or kindness as a result of the long years of agony that they endured under the previous administration.

> "I am therefore," he said to them, "trying to prick their consciences." In the latter part of my time in Addis Ababa, I was fortunate enough to receive a positive response from President Meles Zenawi of Ethiopia in response to my request for an interview.

On October 17th, the appointment was scheduled to take place at 2:30 p.m. at the President's Office, which was located near the Ghion Hotel, where I was staying at the time.

Dr. Abdi Aden, the vice minister of health, provided me with a ride, and I was accompanied by Adam Osman, the former head of Radio Ethiopia's Somali Service, who was with me for the majority of my time in the country. Once we got to the presidency, we had to go through a stringent security check at the main gate, and then we were subjected to another check within the main building. They requested that we provide them with my passport and Adam's identification card, but they did not provide them until after the interview.

The soldiers, who were made up of members of the EPRDF army, were kind but extremely precise. We were able to visit the president without having to wait for a very long time once we entered the premises. The man who was wearing a two-piece grey suit and a tie, Mr. Zenawi, is not a particularly tall individual.

He is almost the same height as I am, which is 5 feet 6-7 inches. In spite of being a revolutionary, he was quite courteous and congenial. Initially, I was quite anxious, but as time went on, I became more at ease and even had the guts to ask the president to move seats and sit closer to me.

The president would allow me to place my Sony cassette recorder on a table in front of me. President Zenawi had a solid command of the English language. Although he had spent half of his adult life fighting in the bush against Col. Mengistu's tremendous army, Meles Zenawi spoke English that was superior to mine, although I had lived in London for more than twenty years. Our conversation centred on the Oromo Liberation Front's decision to withdraw from the transitional administration as well as the Parliament. The president informed me that this decision did not negatively impact the state's safety or the efficiency of its operations.

Within the government, the OLF held a total of twelve seats in parliament and four cabinet members. As a result of the fact that the Oromos constitute about half of the total population of Ethiopia, many people, including myself, believed that the Ethiopian government would be unable to function efficiently in the absence of the OLF. Nevertheless, the president informed me that there had been peace and tranquilly throughout the nation. Other Oromos from the Oromo People's Democratic Organisation, which is a component of the EPRDF, were appointed to fill the four positions that the OLF held in the cabinet.

Although his administration is unable to provide them with any significant economic assistance, President Meles has stated that it is appealing to the international community for assistance on behalf of the half-million Somali refugees who are currently residing in Ethiopia.

However, the most important thing that he stressed was that his government will make every effort to safeguard the honour and dignity of the proud Somali people. After one week, I boarded a plane and departed Addis for Dire Dawa, which is located in eastern Ethiopia. I was on my way to the Ogaden.

We left Dire Dawa for Jigjiga by road at dawn on October 7, stopping briefly at the ancient town of Harar. We'd have reached Jigjiga in under two hours if the roads weren't so bad. As things stood, we didn't show up until about eight o'clock.

The Erer and Fafan valleys are famous and located between Harar and Jigjiga.

Although it is difficult to adequately describe the splendour of these two valleys, I was reminded of the beautiful scenery of California that has been portrayed in a great number of Hollywood films. One notable distinction, on the other hand, was the large number of camels that I saw grazing contentedly on the hills, giving the impression that they were completely satisfied.

Several British tourists who travelled during the 18th and 19th centuries referred to the two valleys as the most breathtaking places they had ever seen. Following our departure from these valleys, we travelled via the quaint community of Hadow, which is situated at the base of the mountain range known as the Karamardha Mountains.

The next step is to drive rapidly uphill for twenty minutes, and the elevation will allow you to traverse the very large range. Instantaneously, one finds that they are dropping pretty swiftly down, and within a short period of time, their heart is stopped with absolute wonder at the clear view of Jigjiga, which is located approximately seven kilometres distant on a very flat plain whose flora and beauty are astounding.

Part Three
SOMALIA'S MEDIA LANDSCAPE

During the Ogaden War of 1977, which was fought between Somalia and Ethiopia, this region became famous for being the location of the greatest tank combat that ever took place. There were still remnants of several tanks that had been destroyed at the entrance, and one can still see them now.

The town of Dagahbur, which was founded by British colonialists more than eight decades ago, was the destination of our journey, which began in Jigjiga. Dagahbur, which is located in the middle of the Ogaden peninsula, has traditionally been a hub for commercial activity. It is also one of the few towns in the region that is populated by Somalis from all over the country.

During my trip to Dagahbur, I saw several trucks delivering products to Mogadishu, which is currently experiencing a war, as well as to Hargeisa, which is located in Somaliland, and Bosaso, which is located in the north-east. Under the previous government, Dagahbur, which has a population of over sixty thousand, including nearly twenty thousand refugees from war-torn Somalia, did not have any hospitals, schools, or educational institutions. As a result of this neglect, the Ogaden area of Somalia has become one of the most backwards regions in the country.

In spite of this, the region does not lack any natural resources. There is a massive natural gas reservoir that was recently discovered close to the town of Shilabo, which is located not too far from the border with central Somalia. This is in addition to the region's long history of abundant livestock.

Recent construction of an amazing health centre in Dagahbur was carried out by the authorities of the EPRDF. And although patients have expressed their dissatisfaction with the lack of available medications, I am confident that this will eventually lead to an improvement in the overall quality of health in the community. Furthermore, the rainy season is when this region of Ethiopia is at its most breathtakingly gorgeous. Over the course of more than three decades, the journey that I took between Dire Dawa and Dagah-

Bur, which is around three hundred kilometres in length, was the most challenging one I have ever experienced.

The road was the worst I have ever seen, and although we had a strong Toyota Land Cruiser, which was driven by Dr. Mengistu Asnake, the head of Eastern Hararghe's Health Administration, it was not able to compensate for the road.

A substantial road development project will be initiated in the region, according to the EPRDF government, which has promised to do so. If this comes to pass, I have no doubt that the economic lives of the people would undergo a significant transformation in a brief amount of time.

People from Europe frequently use the term "desert" to describe the Ogaden.

On the other hand, this description is nothing short of entirely wrong. As a matter of fact, the sun's heat causes the ground to turn yellow when there is no rain present. It only takes a little bit of rain for the entire region to convert into a verdant paradise. While travelling between Jigjiga and Dagah-Bur, I observed a great number of wild animals, including warthogs, digdig, and many groups of forest pheasants.

The regional and local elections in the Somali-inhabited regions of Ethiopia were poised to provide Ethiopian Somalis with the rightful political representation they have long sought since the transfer of control over the Somali territories, including the Ogaden and Reserved areas, to the late Emperor Haile Selassie's government by Great Britain in 1948.

> In 1995, a nation experiences multiple phases of development over its lifespan, and I contend that the Ethiopian Somalis have yet to initiate their economic journey. It required many years before they could be considered to have progressed beyond the initial stages, much less to a point of significant advancement.

Part Three
SOMALIA'S MEDIA LANDSCAPE

The progression encompasses crawling, ambulation, and ultimately ascending to soar towards a realm of aspiration, where individuals are empowered to pursue elevated ideals.

I contended that the Ethiopian Somalis have yet to initiate their economic journey, and it requires a considerable span of time before one can even consider the prospect of advancement, much less significant progress. To accomplish this, a substantial infusion of capital would be necessary to actualise their objectives. The persistent enquiry, naturally, revolves around who possesses the capability or willingness to furnish the necessary capital for the region's urgent economic advancement.

My professional journey to Ethiopia was among the most fruitful endeavours I had ever undertaken. During my time there, I successfully conducted numerous interviews addressing political, economic, social, and cultural matters, engaging not only with Somalis but also with various ministers, including President Meles Zenawi.

The interviews, conducted in English, were subsequently broadcast by the World Service's News. Moreover, Network Africa has utilised multiple interviews from that period. "Section 5" will continue broadcasting the Somali interviews, which have been presented for over a month.

4.2: PROHIBITON OF IMPORT, PRODUCTION, SALE, AND CONSUMPTION

After recognising the negative impact of khat chewing on health and the nation's socioeconomic development, Somalia's national authorities passed a law on March 18, 1983, that outlawed the importation, cultivation, commerce, and consumption of khat. The anti-khat campaign and the resulting ban on khat are considered one of Somalia's most important achievements in recent history, and they have produced outstanding effects.

The 1983 legislation was not the initial instance of a law against khat being implemented. In 1921 and 1939, the cultivation, importation, and possession of khat were prohibited. In the same vein, the importation and possession of khat were prohibited in 1956.

The public's lack of awareness regarding the dangers of khat-chewing and the low level of conformance with these laws resulted in their failure to yield any results. Another contributing factor to their failure was the absence of a viable khat control programme.

The 1983 law was enacted under significantly more favourable conditions. The public was cognisant of the issue, and numerous individuals anticipated the implementation of robust measures to combat the consumption of khat..

4.2.1: Enforcement of the 1983 prohibition statute

It was evident that the law alone was insufficient to address a profoundly ingrained habit of khat chewing. Therefore, the law was merely the initial stage in a series of measures that have been implemented to regulate khat. An essential part of carrying out the law's enforcement was creating a thorough national programme to regulate the drug's consumption, importation, cultivation, and trade. In reality, the law's promulgation was immediately followed by:

a) The establishment of khat committees at the national, regional, and municipal levels;
b) A mass media-based information and education campaign;
c) The organisation of, and active participation in, national and international meetings regarding the issues of khat.

In summary, the entire nation was mobilised to assist in the effective implementation of the law's provisions. The principal authority responsible for the regulation of khat is the National Committee for the Eradication of Khat. The Committee is composed of prominent political and state figures. Regularly,

the Committee convenes twice a month. Its primary obligations include:
a) To guarantee the enforcement of the prohibition law;
b) To establish and sustain a khat control system;
c) To implement educational and informational campaigns about the risks linked to khat consumption.

To offer recreational facilities that serve as healthful alternatives to khat sessions;
a) To coordinate the regulation of narcotic drugs, psychotropic substances, and other psychoactive substances, as well as khat eradication initiatives;
b) to harmonise the efforts of diverse khat committees, including the National Research Committee on Khat and regional and local khat eradication committees;
c) To ensure a uniform dissemination of information pertaining to khat control.

The implementation of the 1983 Act necessitated the reallocation of national resources to fulfil its aims. A multitude of problems emerged; nonetheless, the team confronted these challenges with steadfast resolve. The primary issue was the harm inflicted on farmers due to the devastation of khat crops. Prior to the demolition, they conducted a thorough evaluation of the khat cultivation region and the quantity of khat trees on each farm. Regrettably, the anticipated procedures for sufficient compensation of farmers' losses were not discerned.

The available local resources were inadequate for the required technical and financial assistance. This situation has elicited much apprehension, and resolutions are still being pursued.

An additional issue necessitating addressing was the unemployment generated among individuals previously engaged in the khat trade. All endeavours were undertaken to assist them and direct their energies towards constructive and socially acceptable pursuits. A surge in demand arose for recreational facilities providing healthier alternatives to khat gatherings, a prevalent form of social interaction

4.3: ACHIEVEMENTS

The opposition to the prohibition bill was met with overwhelmingly positive responses from the general population. Following the implementation of the new law, a sense of hope emerged, which immediately replaced the previously common feeling of frustration. Despite this, there were some segments of the population who voiced their opposition to the prohibition because of the income they received from the khat trade or because they were dependent on it.

These individuals opposed the steps that were taken to combat khat and attempted to import the substance illegally into the country through various different means. Because of the ongoing implementation of the legislation and the progressive intensification of the anti-khat campaign, however, their disruptive activities became increasingly unsustainable.

As a consequence of this, the nation's imports of khat experienced a large decrease, particularly in regions that were geographically remote from the supply sources in neighbouring countries. Although only trace amounts of khat are still being brought into the nation illegally, the price of this substance has increased by 15 to 25 times in comparison to what it was worth before the prohibition.

The result of this is that the objectives of the prohibition act have been completely accomplished in the vast majority of locations across the country. Although khat is no longer openly used in many areas, particularly near the borders, there are still some small quantities that are being smuggled and used illegally.

There is a significant variation in the degree to which individuals who have given up the practice of chewing khat see improvements in their social, economic, and health circumstances. It is clear that the problems that are associated with chewing khat, such as the disruption of familial ties and the violation of public ethics, are becoming less prevalent in certain locations. The amount of hard currency spent on khat acquisition has dropped significantly, as shown by the large decrease in the total amount of khat brought into the country.

The facts presented above provide support for the conclusion that the khat eradication effort and its utilisation, which were carried out in conformity with the prohibition statute of 1983, have been successful.

4.3.1: The Case of Khat Between East African Nations

In response to the emergence of Covid in Somalia in 2019, President Mohamed Abdullahi Farmajo mandated a cessation and prohibition of khat imports from Kenya to Somalia. Nevertheless, the case has impacted the relationship between Somalia and Kenya, as the khat business had a significant impact on khat farmers in Kenya. (BBC News, 14 May 2020)

Khat has become an essential element of livelihoods in Kenyan regions, offering farmers greater returns than tea and coffee. In 2022, Somalia became a notable market for Kenyan khat, with daily shipments totaling 19 tons, leading to considerable financial benefits amounting to billions of shillings.

Despite the ban on Kenyan khat, there have been some speculations that instead the khat imports were moved to an Ethiopian business where businessmen started importing from Ethiopia. The move caused tension in the relationship between Kenya and Ethiopia.

In July 2022, President Hassan Sheekh Mohamud consented to revoke the ban on air freighting khat from Kenya, which was enforced for over two years. The decision, which comes a day after Kenyan President Uhuru Kenyatta traveled to Mogadishu to attend the inauguration of Hassan Sheikh Mohamoud as the new president of Somalia, represents a thawing of the two countries' tense relations under former President Mohamed Abdullahi Farmajo.

In this precarious situation, Mogadishu revoked the prohibition on the air shipment of miraa, also known as khat, from Kenya, which was instituted in March 2020 due to the coronavirus pandemic.

During the same timeframe, Kenyan Agriculture Minister Peter Munya declared that the two countries had completed their trade agreements. Under one of these agreements, Somalia would export fish and other items to Kenya, while Kenya will be able to restart exporting miraa, a plant that is highly valued in Somalia for its stimulant and appetite-suppressant qualities. He declared that these agreements would be executed "within two weeks."

The prohibition has severely impacted central Kenya, where 50 tons of miraa valued at 6 million shillings ($50,000) were exported to Somalia daily, as stated by Kimathi Munjuri, secretary general of a prominent miraa producers' association.

Certain European nations categorised khat as a narcotic. Despite having a 700-kilometer border and being supposedly allies in the fight against the Shabab Islamists, Kenya and Somalia continue to have a tense relationship.

Somalia has consistently alleged that Kenya is interfering, whereas Kenya has accused Mogadishu of attempting to find a scapegoat for its domestic issues.

Somalia terminated diplomatic relations with Kenya in December 2020, following Uhuru Kenyatta's hosting of the president of the unrecognised self-proclaimed country of Somaliland, which Mogadishu regards as an essential part of Somalia. They were reinstated in August 2021.

The determination of the two countries' maritime borders in the Indian Ocean is the subject of a dispute. In October 2021, Somalia was granted a massive 100,000 km^2 region that is abundant in fish and may contain hydrocarbons by the International Court of Justice, the principal court of the United Nations.

Part Three
SOMALIA'S MEDIA LANDSCAPE

According to government data released in May, Kenya exported 13 billion shillings to Somalia in 2021, which represented 5% of its total exports to African countries and exceeded $110 million.

4.4: KHAT SPEECH: KHAT, (CATHA EDULIS)

In this part I will cover khat history, chemical composition, and the effect on people who use st.

I was deeply honoured and privileged to have been invited to the conference where the topic of narcotics was addressed. In addition, I took the opportunity to convey my profound appreciation to the Swedish National Board of Health and Welfare for inviting me to Stockholm, the capital of this magnificent nation, to discuss khat, a stimulant plant that is extensively employed in the Arab Republic of Yemen and East Africa. Its botanical name is Catha edulis.

I was particularly grateful to Mr. Abdikarim Ali, the general manager of the Somali Swedish Development and Relief Association, the Somali Women in Sweden, and the other organisations in Sweden that recommended my name for inclusion on the conference invitation list. Ali Darwish was the individual who contacted me in April to inform me that the National Board of Health and Welfare was considering inviting me to speak at the conference. When they finally extended the invitation, I gratefully accepted it, and he continued to communicate with me until my arrival yesterday evening. Nevertheless, I would like to provide a brief overview of Somalia's geographic location and population for those who are not already acquainted with the country.

Somalia is located in the Horn of Africa, a region of the East African coast that spans 637,657 square kilometres. It is believed to have the longest seacoast in Africa, second only to South Africa, and its population is estimated to be between 8 and 11 million. I initiated a conversation regarding the history, chemical composition, and impact of khat on its users.

Catha edulis, a green stimulant plant, is commonly referred to as khat, qaat, or jaad in East Africa. It is primarily cultivated in Western Kenya, Ethiopia, and the Arab Republic of Yemen. However, it is extensively employed in the Horn of Africa, with a particular emphasis on Somalia and the Republic of Djibouti on the Red Sea Coast, as well as the Arab Republic of Yemen. It is also recognised in Tanzania, Uganda, and the Eastern Congo.

Additionally, it was determined that khat is cultivated in Zambia, Malawi, Zimbabwe, and South Africa, where it is known by various names. For example, in Uganda, it is referred to as mutabangwa or musty. In Tanzania, where khat is prohibited, it is referred to as Burundi, warfa, and other terms. In South Africa, it is referred to as bushman's tea.

In Uganda and Tanzania, khat is a commonly used substance, with the majority of users hailing from the coastal cities of Kenya or Somalia. More than eight hundred years ago, khat was first discovered in Kenya and Eastern Ethiopia, around the ancient city of Harar, according to various reports chronicled by Arab travellers, primarily in East Africa during the 12th century.

From there, it proceeded to Yemen, as we will observe in the future. The existence of khat, as indicated by its botanic name, Catha edulis, dates back several thousandyears. The term "catha edulis" is derived from the Greek word "edulis," which means edible. Consequently, the term "catha edulis" refers to the "edible plant." For instance, archaeologists and researchers in South Africa assert that the use of khat in the country dates back more than two millennia.

However, I had not encountered any documentary evidence to support this claim in the limited research on khat in South Africa. Northern Somalia, which is now referred to as Somaliland, and the Republic of Djibouti, both of which share a lengthy border with Ethiopia. Khat arrived in the area approximately one hundred years ago. Khat is a plant that thrives in cold, high altitudes. It is primarily found on mountain slopes, typically at an elevation of over four thousand feet above sea level, as well as at ground level.

The branches of this plant can be developed to a height of 18 metres. The finest and most stimulating khat is grown in Kenya and Ethiopia, both of which are situated at an elevation of over four thousand feet above sea level.

4.4.1: Kenyan Mira Khat

Spending hundreds of thousands of dollars daily, Somalia, Djibouti, and the Northeastern Province of Kenya—a place where Somalis make up the majority—import massive amounts of khat from Ethiopia and Kenya. As an example, the small, impoverished nation of Djibouti spends more than $200,000 per day on importing this verdant plant from Ethiopia's eastern highlands while having a population of less than 500,000. Awaday, a town approximately 10 km north of Harar, is home to their preferred kind. They claim this variety is more potent than others found in Ethiopia.

Khat grown in the town of Mero in western Kenya is far more potent than the Ethiopian varieties, and its fans in central and southern Somalia shell out more than $300,000 daily to get their hands on it. Several southern towns, including the capital Mogadishu, see as many as fifty light Cessna planes touch down every day just before midday. After a few hours, nearly everyone in Mogadishu, a city of over a million people, is either napping or chewing miro. Plus, this nation lacked a functional central government for almost 16 years following General Mohamed Siyad Barre's revolutionary regime's overthrow.

> Khat Effects: Khat has a bitter taste, and like alcohol, a first-time user finds it quite bitter and very disagreeable and often wonders why anybody would bother to chew these leaves, like goats, which have no use at all other than making one

restless and feeling agoraphobic, but after a while one gets used to it and enjoys chewing it.

The delicate branches and shoots are gathered in varying lengths and widths and then chewed for extended periods of time, typically in chambers filled with smoke, which can last up to twelve hours. Although the individual experiences euphoria and relaxation in the initial hours, they may experience high blood pressure and possibly depression by the session's conclusion. It can induce psychosis or severe depression if chewed for an extended period of time and can be addictive. Despite its relative insufficiency compared to other narcotics, it remains illegal in the United States, the majority of Europe, and the United Kingdom. Although most of these countries—including Sweden—permitted its sale, a significant amount of khat nonetheless managed to get through Holland.

The first book on khat was written in 1237 by an Egyptian historian and traveller named Nasias Samaraqandi, according to a Somali author residing in Saudi Arabia named Mohamed Abdi-Daud, who published a book on the subject in 1998. It was used locally to alleviate melancholy and depression because "it induces relaxation and excitement," according to Samarqandi. Kilwa was an old name for Kenya. Another author, likely of Yemeni descent, Ibnu Fadlillahi Al-Amiri, wrote about it in 1342; he called it an "Abyssinian Plant," an old term for Ethiopia.

Chewing on its delicate leaves, he claims, provides «stimulation and makes him relax.» Chewers, he notes, tend to lose interest in food and sleep, which could be a benefit for folks who have to travel a lot or work a lot.

Harar had been the centre of Islamic scholarship for almost a thousand years, until the renowned British adventurer and writer Richard Burton became the first European to set foot in the city in 1854.

Part Three
SOMALIA'S MEDIA LANDSCAPE

A skilled linguist who spoke classical Arabic well (one of his seven languages), Burton introduced himself to the city's ruling clerics as Sheikh Abdulla and claimed to be from the Saudi holy city of Makka. According to Burton, the residents of Harar City indulged in heavy khat use, beginning at 9 in the morning and continuing until approximately noon, when they would scatter to attend the mosque for the midday (zuhur) prayer, which often takes place at 12:30 in the afternoon. They would gather and resume chewing until nightfall following prayer and a brief lunch. He mentioned that each person used a little wooden ball, which was somewhat bigger than an egg, to crush the leaves.

Because khat erodes gums and causes teeth to fall out, it's safe to assume that most of them lacked teeth; therefore, the leaves made chewing easier. After a day of revelry, these folks make their way home in the evening. According to Burton, the lords of Harar informed him that they thought it was "Food for Saints" (Quutul awliya in Arabic). The drowsiness and calmness they experience while eating it allow them to recite the Qur'an for extended periods of time. According to Burton, who put the Harar population at roughly 8,000, khat originated in Harar and made its way to Yemen some 700 years ago.

A local legend states that Sheikh Abadir Muse, a Muslim saint from Harar town in the early 12th century, brought khat to the town's inhabitants. He advised those who wanted to recite the Qu'ran at night to chew the green leaves, and the majority of Harar people still relish the taste of the leaves, more than 800 years after the original story was told. The town's Saint's Tomb receives hundreds of visitors daily who come to pray and pay their respects. An article about Somali immigrants' use of khat in the United States from Newsweek's October–December 2002 issue asserted that religious leaders in the Ottoman Empire chewed it while reading the Qur'an for days on end. Maybe such an event took place in Harar, which was under Ottoman control in the early 17th century along with the surrounding area. The building blocks: The National Criminal Intelligence Service (NCIS) of Britain says that the main components of khat are alkaloids, cathinone, and cathine, which are similar in structure and function to amphetamine and have similar stimulating effects on the central nervous system.

According to NCIS, the drug's effects are comparable to that of a five-milligramme amphetamine dose and can endure for up to twenty-four hours.

They noted that chewers experience a decrease in appetite and sleepiness, suggesting that this could be beneficial for individuals who have lengthy travels or work shifts. Cathinone H. D., whose full name she chose not to reveal, is a 29-year-old mother of one whose marriage ended in divorce due to her husband's insistence on continuing to smoke khat. She claims that khat is the primary reason many Somali immigrant marriages in Britain fail; she invested significant effort to train her husband to be a better provider for their family, but she had to make numerous concessions because, despite being a strong woman, she needed support. She insisted that he chew khat exclusively at home, where she could keep a close watch on him. However, he would silently wake up in the early hours of the morning, seeking others who shared his habit.

Arriving home in the morning, he would be utterly worn out and untidy. Then, without uttering a word, he would collapse onto the bed, leaving him tormented by hunger and a lack of direction until late at night. She eventually insisted he pick between his second wife, khat, and himself, his devoted wife. He left his family and immediately married his second wife. After promising herself she would never tie the knot with another khat addict, H.D. remained single for a while.

Yemenis and Ethiopians are the three main ethnic groups in the UK that produce and trade khat. The majority of khat sales occur in London, but demand is highest in the regions where these populations have settled.

Part Three
SOMALIA'S MEDIA LANDSCAPE

The area includes the Midlands, the North-east, the Northwest, Scotland, and Wales, especially Cardiff, where a sizeable Somali population resides. Khat plants gathered in Ethiopia's Eastern Highlands or Western Kenya's border regions are prepared for sale in the Netherlands and the United Kingdom the very next day, all thanks to the remarkably effective transportation networks. According to NCIS, Heathrow Airport imported around seven tonnes of khat weekly before the prohibition. Heathrow, along with other UK airports like Gatwick and Manchester, was a common point of collection for over 80 khat importers who routinely made use of airfreight capabilities.

Reported profits from the sale of khat in the UK during those days vary, but as a rough estimate, two thousand bundles of khat might have been acquired in Kenya for a thousand pounds. Airfreight to the UK costs around £300, and individual bundles are sold in London for £4. The overall consignment generates £8000, representing a six hundred and fifteen percent increase over the retailer's initial investment. Legal Status: Cathinone and cathine were not subject to the Misuse of Drugs Act 1971 (Class C) at the time. An offence occurs only when one isolates the active elements of the plant

The UK outlawed miraa/khat on June 24, 2014. This change comes after the British Parliament approved the government's decision to categorise khat as a class C narcotic, making it unlawful to supply, possess with the intent to supply, or import. The penalties for these Class C drug offences are up to 14 years in jail, an infinite fine, or both.

4.4.2: Khat Ban in Somalia

In 1983, the government of the late President Mohamed Siyad Barre of Somalia enacted legislation prohibiting the importation, sale, or consumption of khat in Somalia. Prior to the prohibition, he addressed the nation at a public rally at Mogadishu's Soccer

Stadium, outlining the severe economic and social effects of khat on Somali society.

He claimed that a significant portion of the country's limited hard currency, which was critically required for development, was spent on importing khat leaves from Kenya and Ethiopia. He went on to say that khat encouraged corruption, theft from the public coffers, vices like prostitution, and clan fighting. Most importantly, he maintained that khat was harmful to human health. Because of these critical elements, he declared, 'We must act quickly and ban it.' A few days later, the banning decree was officially published and broadcast on state radio and television.

4.5: SOMALI ARMY ENGAGED IN KHAT SMUGGLING

The initial restriction on the import of leaves did not prevent many people from sneaking them into the country after a few months of its implementation. According to reputable sources, these included top leaders in the then-national army, who used personnel carriers and other army trucks to collect sacks packed with khat from the Kenyan border, which were transported there by rented Kenyan-registered cars.

Frequently, unsuspecting members of the police and security services, stationed at roadblocks seeking khat smugglers, passed these army trucks carrying illegal goods. Even if security forces knew trucks were smuggling drugs into the country, they couldn't stop them. Automatic machine guns would have ambushed them if they had attempted to stop.

The contraband was immediately transported to southern locations, including Mogadishu, and sold under the counter to some cabinet ministers in bundles retailing in London for £4. The overall consignment generates £8000, representing a six hundred and fifteen percent increase over the retailer's initial investment.

In an October 2002 edition of Newsweek Magazine, a piece on khat difficulties among Somali immigrants in the United States was published under the title 'Coming to America.' It stated that khat has been prohibited in the United States since 1993. Because of the increase in immigration, it is moving up the authorities' watch lists of new substances. It goes on to say that the Somali populations in Minneapolis and Columbus, Ohio, for example, have increased from a few hundred in the early 1990s to approximately 40,000 and 30,000, respectively.

According to Newsweek, between 2002 and 2005, US Customs inspectors nearly doubled their khat seizures. In August 2002, the Columbus Despatch, a daily published in Columbus, Ohio, reported that a Somali man had become the first person in Ohio to be sentenced on khat possession charges. At Lancaster's South-Eastern Correctional Institution, he is currently serving a ten-year sentence. According to the newspaper, the United States government seized 82,000 pounds of khat in 2001, more than doubling the amount confiscated in 1996. United States Drug Enforcement Administration (DEA): A DEA report indicates that khat is illegal in the United States, yet it incorrectly claims that it is legal in many parts of Europe. It notes that individuals of East African and Middle Eastern descent are often responsible for the importation, distribution, possession, or use of khat in the US.

The DEA conducted 'Operation Somalia Express' in July 2006, an 18-month investigation that resulted in the coordinated arrest of a 44-member international trafficking organisation responsible for smuggling more than 25 tonnes of khat (estimated by the DEA to be worth more than $10 million) from the Horn of Africa to the United States.

Khat plays a significant role in the economies of several producer countries, notably Kenya, Ethiopia, and Yemen. Reports from Yemen indicate that Yemenis allocate over US$2 billion each year for the purchase of khat, which is frequently cultivated on land that is not viable for alternative crops.

4.5.1: Yemeni khat from the town of Taiz

The only known case of khat cultivation in the United States occurred in September 1998, when 1,076 plants were seized in a raid in Salinas, California. Sophisticated irrigation techniques were used; the individual involved was of Middle Eastern origin and was earning approximately US$10,000 per month. The DEA did not disclose the specific actions taken against the individual. I understand that, despite this spirited and efficient action by the DEA to fight against the importation and sale of the green stimulant plant in the USA, the stuff can still be bought under the table in several American cities where immigrants from East Africa and the Arabian Peninsula live.

A Somali Islamic charity organisation based in Riyadh, the Saudi capital, recorded and disseminated cassettes inside and outside Somalia some years ago containing a message strongly condemning the use of khat among the Somalis. The message is the result of long research by the organisation on the detrimental health effects of khat on people who use it.

The message says that khat is a dangerous drug that ruins many family lives and creates endless strife and clan warfare in Somali society. It says that Islam forbids anything that may stimulate, such as drugs, or intoxicate or inebriate the human brain, such as alcohol. The message also carries a Somali poem about the negative effect of khat on people.

4.5.2: Here Is A Summary of It

a) Oh khat, you induce a faraway state of mind in people.
b) How many have you deluded into building castles in the air?
c) How many established marriages have you destroyed? To how many families' lives have you turned to utter misery?
d) To how many did you give paranoia and depression?
e) To how many did you give nightmares, sleeplessness, and exhaustion?

f) How many appetites did you kill, and how many lost their desire to live?
g) In how many did you induce uncontrollable aggression?
h) How many did you make impotent and unwanted?

'Oh khat, you give people all these and many more problems . And yet people continue to poison their bodies and minds with your unhealthy and poisonous 'juice'.

4.5.3: A Debate On Khat Held In West London

A few years ago, a friend of mine, Ahmed Sheekh, and I organised a debate on the social, health, and economic impacts of khat on the people who use it in West London.

Users and non-users of khat have both attended the debate, which was sometimes very heated. Those who chewed the green plant were very strong in their defence, whereas those who didn't were equally strong in their opposition to it.

Dr. Yassin Mohamed, a microbiologist who had spoken several times at other khat-related meetings about the health hazards of the green drug, was a guest speaker. Dr. Yassin spoke at length about khat's detrimental effect on the health of users. He says that if khat is chewed, as often happens, in overcrowded rooms, where doors and windows are firmly shut, with the chewers also continuously smoking, people can easily get diseases, such as diarrhoea, flu, constipation, and even tuberculosis.

Dr. Yassin said that the increasing use of pesticides on khat plantations by producer countries poses serious health problems for khat users. He strongly recommends that khat chewers wash the stuff thoroughly before chewing it to remove any pesticide residue, which otherwise might get into their system and might gradually cause them some serious harm.

Two other guests, Adan Jama and Mohamed Kooreeye, who both used khat, defended chewing it and insisted that it was a good pastime. They said that khat is often used when people gather to solve clan conflicts or financial disputes or have discussions about arranging marriages or solving problems relating to them, such as separation or divorce.

Mr. Jama argued that khat does not give him any problems at all, and after 30 years of continuous chewing, he never had any exhaustion, mental fatigue, or insomnia. He added that after chewing khat, he always slept soundly. The only time he has any such complications is when he misses his usual diet of khat-chewing sessions in the evenings!

Another speaker, Mohamed Mohamoud, said he stopped chewing the green stimulant leaves a few years ago, after using them for nearly twenty years. He said he felt that starting the habit of chewing khat was the worst mistake he had ever made in his life, and for a long time, he says he led the life of a tramp, avoiding all his relatives and close friends so that they didn't see the utterly miserable life he was living.

Mr. Mohamoud had a word of advice for khat chewers.

He tells them that it is still not too late to stop it, but he particularly reserves his strongest warning for the young Somali men and women who might be contemplating starting.

He says they should avoid taking up the habit at all costs.

If they did not heed his advice, he said, they would ruin not only their lives but also their health quite irreparably—something they would regret for the rest of their lives, as he did, he added.

4.5.4: My Speech on the Day I Was Receiving ISA 2019 Award: A Lifetime Achievement Awards

I felt honoured, humbled, and genuinely moved to receive this renowned medal, which I preserved and treasured for as long as I lived.

I was also very proud to be here among the people to celebrate the 4th International Somali Awards ceremony, which has brought together Somalis from all walks of life and aims to recognise

Part Three
SOMALIA'S MEDIA LANDSCAPE

many special individuals who have positively contributed to the progress of the Somali people socially, economically, and culturally. A group of cultivated Somalis, predominantly living in the Diaspora, founded the International Somali Awards. The beauty of the event was that the Somalis themselves created and sponsored it, recognising and appreciating the amazing achievements of their own people.

I believed if other like-minded Somalis got together with their positive ideas and financial contributions, Somalia would make rapid progress in all fields.

The cruel and brutal civil war destroyed Somalia, claiming the lives of hundreds of thousands of Somalis and, as a result, forcing more than one and a half million people, mostly young men and women with children, to flee and seek refuge in foreign lands, where many of them were treated cruelly and were living in miserable conditions in refugee camps. If the Somali youth had united and worked together, the disintegration of Somalia would probably never have taken place. As the wise saying goes, "A house divided against itself does not stand; it ends in utter ruins."

The International Somalia Awards had previously invited and recognised highly distinguished Somalis. This opportunity allowed me to mention two individuals who, in my opinion, have made significant contributions to the Somali people: Dr. Hawo Abdi and Dahabshiil, the well-known Somali money transferring agency. Dr. Hawo established the 'Drs. Hawo Abdi Foundation,' which operates a camp and hospital that provides food, education, and medical care to displaced and underprivileged people. She constructed her hospital in 'Ceelasha Biyaha,' often known as Water Wells, a location between Mogadishu and Afgoye, an area where many Somalis have been living in deplorable conditions.

One day, a group of criminal gangsters attacked her hospital with the intention of destroying it completely. However, they underestimated Dr. Hawo, who, instead of fleeing to save her life, stood up to fight off these mindless criminals. They did some damage to the hospital and the sick people who were treated there, but they were chased away, and the hospital was saved.

Dr. Hawo was praised by the world for building the hospital and for resisting those who wanted to deny food and care to the sick and starving Somalis.

The other person is Mr. Abdirashid Duale, the chairman of Dahabshiil Group. Mr. Abdirashid Duale's company had been sending remittances to many hundreds of thousands of Somalis, mostly Diasporas who fled their country because of the civil war.

The wonderful thing was that Dahabshiil sent money even in conflict zones and was there during the humanitarian crises.

I was proud to say I was one of those people who benefited from these remittances, as many members of my family were scattered in many parts of Somalia and elsewhere. Personally, I had always been grateful to Dahabshiil.

As a result, I was really pleased to be recognised among these outstanding individuals, and this medal meant a lot to me. I accept this award with heartfelt thanks and humility

4.5.5: What I Have Emphasised

It is very difficult to gauge the exact number of people who use that, as there is no research or statistics that give any accurate number, or at least, I have not seen any.

However, it is estimated that over 20 million people, primarily Muslims, chew khat on a daily basis. The majority of these people are Oromos, the largest ethnic group in Ethiopia (about 30 million), of which at least half are Muslim farmers who live in eastern and

Part Three
Somalia's Media Landscape

southwestern Ethiopia. It is believed that more than 5 million of these Muslim Oromos use khat while working on their farms, doing other business, or reciting the Qu'ran. In some parts of Ethiopia, as the khat business presents significant financial opportunities, some farmers have uprooted their coffee and other plantations to plant khat trees instead.

Over 4 million Somalis residing within Somalia or in the diaspora, with a significant population in eastern Ethiopia and the Republic of Djibouti, alongside more than one hundred thousand Somalis in the northeastern region of Kenya, expend thousands of dollars each day to import khat from Kenya and Ethiopia. Hundreds of thousands of Somalis who live in Eastern Ethiopia also chew khat in fairly large quantities, but I could not establish how much money they spend to buy that.

Contrary to the Oromos in Ethiopia, the Somalis who use khat are predominately civil servants, teachers, soldiers, businessmen, doctors, and artists, as well as nomads and, in Southern Somalia, farmers. In the Republic of Yemen, which has a population of eighteen million, over 80 percent, which is a staggering twelve and a half million of the adult population, spend nearly two billion dollars annually to buy khat, which is almost entirely homegrown.

Unusually, a large number of women are users in Yemen. Khat is a lucrative business for both producers and sellers. Approximately 5 to 6 million individuals derive significant financial gains from khat, whether through its transportation or sale.

Medical men and laboratory analysts have confirmed that most khat users often suffer from various types of illnesses, such as manic depression. To how many did you give nightmares, sleeplessness, and exhaustion? How many appetites did you kill, and how many lost their desire to live?

In how many individuals did you induce uncontrollable aggression?

How many did you make impotent and unwanted? ‹Oh Khat, you give people all these and many more problems. Despite the known dangers, people still choose to poison their bodies and minds with your unhealthy and toxic juice..

Part Five:
Awards & Spe

CHAPTER 5

A DISCOURSE ON KHAT TOOK PLACE IN WEST LONDON

Several years prior, a colleague of mine, Ahmed Sheekh, and I orchestrated a debate concerning the social, health, and economic ramifications of khat on its users in West London. Both proponents and opponents of khat participated in the debate, which at times became quite intense. Those who took the verdant herb exhibited a robust defence, while those who abstained demonstrated an equally vigourous opposition.

Dr. Yassin Mohamed, a microbiologist with a history of addressing the health risks associated with green drugs at various khat-related conferences, served as a guest speaker. Dr. Yassin elab-

Part Five
AWARDS & SPEECH

orated extensively on the adverse health implications associated with khat consumption. He asserts that chewing khat, particularly in densely populated spaces where doors and windows remain tightly sealed, compounded by the constant presence of cigarette smoke, can lead to a heightened risk of various ailments, including diarrhoea, influenza, constipation, and even tuberculosis.

Dr. Yassin articulated that the escalating application of pesticides on khat plantations by producing nations presents significant health concerns for khat consumers. He emphatically advises that individuals who partake in khat should meticulously cleanse the leaves prior to consumption to eliminate any pesticide remnants, which could otherwise infiltrate their system and potentially lead to significant health repercussions over time. Two additional guests, Adan Jama and Mohamed Kooreeye, both of whom partake in khat, articulated their defence of the practice, asserting that it serves as a commendable leisure activity. Khat is frequently used during gatherings, where individuals seek to address clan conflicts or financial disagreements or engage in discussions regarding marriage arrangements and related issues, including separation or divorce.

Mr. Jama contended that khat has not posed any issues for him whatsoever, and after three decades of consistent consumption, he has never experienced exhaustion, mental fatigue, or insomnia. He remarked that he consistently experienced profound slumber following the consumption of khat. His only instances of complications arise when he neglects his customary evening sessions of khat chewing. Another speaker, Mohamed Mohamoud, indicated that he ceased consumption of the green stimulant leaves several years ago, having used them for nearly two decades. He expressed that initiating the habit of chewing khat was the gravest error he had ever committed in his life, and for an extended period, he claims he lived a life akin to that of a vagabond, suffering from constipation, insomnia, bowel inflammation, and, in certain instances, cancer of the mouth and throat. It is often observed that individuals who engage in habitual usage, especially males, frequently struggle with essential activities such as eating, sleeping, or maintaining healthy sexual relationships—three critical components for a fulfilling life.

A considerable number of male khat chewers consume alcohol, predominantly beer or wine, following extended periods of khat chewing to counteract its effects and facilitate sleep. While it is established that khat induces impotence in many men, it conversely appears to enhance sexual desire in women. Several women who regularly partake in khat have, with some hesitation, acknowledged their feelings to me. Nevertheless, when I inquired about their responses to the stimulation of sexual desire, the majority chose not to provide one! Dr. Manton Hirst was the pioneering researcher who conducted an extensive examination of the history of khat in South Africa and authored multiple publications on the subject. During the 1990s, Dr. Hirst was a pioneer in highlighting to the scientific community in South Africa the longstanding use of Catha edulis, a wild tree found in certain areas of the Eastern Cape.

This plant was recognised for its stimulant and medicinal properties by various tribes in the area, the Nguni and, historically, the Khoisan. Archaeologists and researchers in South Africa assert that the use of khat in the region dates back more than two millennia; however, in my limited exploration of the topic, I have encountered no documentary evidence to substantiate this claim. The popularity of khat in South Africa can be attributed to the influx of Somali immigrants who sought refuge there during the 1990s. Individuals from Somalia who previously engaged with khat extensively in their homeland expressed immense satisfaction upon learning that this stimulant plant thrives in the Eastern Cape region.

This knowledge had been largely confined to a select group of elderly residents, aside from the bushmen, who had long used it as an herbal tea, attributing various medicinal properties to it. It has come to my attention that the authorities in South Africa are currently deliberating on the appropriate measures to address the issue of khat consumption. In a parallel vein, numerous Somalis who sought refuge in Australia and New Zealand during the 1990s were equally astonished and pleased to discover the presence of khat in both nations.

Without seeking authorisation from local authorities, they commenced the practice of harvesting the tender branches, engaging in the traditional act of chewing, and occasionally distributing the leaves to fellow khat enthusiasts.

This provoked considerable ire among the police in both nations upon the revelation that their splendid green trees had been ravaged, not by locusts or other pests, but by individuals who had journeyed thousands of miles in search of refuge from a devastating civil war, seeking assistance and solace from the populace and authorities of these lands. NCIS reports on the profitability and legal status of khat importation and sale in the UK.

5.5.1: My Scholarly Investigation: The Prohibition of Khat in Somalia

The utilisation of khat among Somali immigrants residing in the UK is documented in a handbook titled 'You and Your Health,' authored by a Somali women's collective in London, referred to as 'Tawakal.'

Additional perspectives on khat include a scholarly article written by Dr. M.H. Mukhtar, who is a Somali academic at Savannah State University in Georgia, USA.

Kasmo is a Somali newspaper published in London, dedicated to knowledge, with its edition released in April 2002.

a) The Guardian, September 2002, edition
b) Newsweek Magazine, August 2002 issue

A report from the Drug Enforcement Administration (DEA) indicates that khat is banned in the United States. Khat poses a significant threat to human health: a recorded message from a Somali Islamic charity organisation located in Riyadh, Saudi Arabia.

5.1: CONCLUSION

As I started with my writing, I had a long career as a broadcaster. Ethiopian radio has employed me since the 1950s. I went on to the BBC World Service extension after that. The Somali language branch began in the 1950s, and I became one of the staff members working in that branch of the BBC.

As I said, I began working as a broadcaster for the BBC Somali Service at the start of the late 1950s. The British Broadcasting Corporation (BBC) is not only the largest but also the most well-known broadcasting system in the world. Globally, the BBC Somali Service has been regarded as the gold standard among Somali-speaking people. I used to make it a point to work the BBC's daily shows.

The great bulk of adult life would slowly stop if one focused on the radio box. By the 190s, I had become a passionate listener of the Somali service and all other Somali-speaking radio programming.

The richness of daily world news coverage, the classical and, when required, creative vocabulary, and, most importantly, the beautifully appealing voices of the presenters who had a gift for blending simple tonality and clear audibility appropriate for the kind of programme or news item were all distinguishing features. I started to participate in those activities, which were fantastic and improved my broadcasting abilities.

I joined the staff in charge of getting ready for the most delicate programmes, including interviews with notable people. These duties turned into the foundation of my ability.

Starting in 1922, the BBC's radio broadcasts maintained first control over the airwaves. Even today, radio broadcasts continue to play a significant role in the company's operations. Although the UK did not issue any additional broadcasting licences until 1973, foreign commercial competitors began to emerge shortly thereafter. Somalian BBC News was set in the early 1950s when Somalis were struggling for independence from the colonial powers. (BBC, 18 October 1922)

Part Five
AWARDS & SPEECH

As said above, I started my broadcasting career at the Ethiopian radio station. The BBC's radio broadcasts began in 1922. The General Post Office of the British Government, which held original control over the airwaves, granted licences to the BBC because the law once regarded them as an extension of Post Office services. Radio broadcasts still account for a significant portion of the corporation's output today, as indicated by the name of the BBC listings. This system is the basis for modern mass media communication technology.

I wrote my memories for our future generation.

Abdullahi Haji
My Life Through News Media

IMAGE 1:
The author Abdulahi Haji

IMAGE 2:
From left to right: the author Abdulahi Haji

Part Five
AWARDS & SPEECH

IMAGE 3:
The author Abdulahi Haji

IMAGE 4:
The author Abdulahi Haji.

IMAGE 5:
From left to right: the author Abdulahi Haji

IMAGE 6:
The author Abdulahi Haji

Part Five
AWARDS & SPEECH

IMAGE 7:
From left to right: the author Abdulahi Haji

IMAGE 8:
From left to right: Asha , the author Abdulahi Haji, and Ambassador Sharif Salah.

Abdullahi Haji
My Life Through News Media

IMAGE 9:
The author Abdulahi Haji

IMAGE 10:
The author Abdulahi Haji

Part Five
AWARDS & SPEECH

IMAGE 11:
From left to right: the author Abdulahi Haji

IMAGE 12:
From left to right: the author Abdulahi Haji, the then Somali President Mohamed Siad Barre.

Abdullahi Haji
My Life Through News Media

IMAGE 13:

IMAGE 14:
From left to right: , , the author Abdulahi Haji

Part Five
Awards & Speech

IMAGE 15:
From left to right: Former minister of higher education Abdisalam Sheikh Hussein and the author Abdulahi Haji.

IMAGE 16:
From left to right: the author Abdulahi Haji

Abdullahi Haji
My Life Through News Media

IMAGE 17:
From left to right seated: One of the editors, former Ambassador Ahmed Sh. Mohamud, the author Abdulahi Haji, and Ambassador Abdirashid Seed.

IMAGE 18:
The author Abdulahi Haji, nominated and won the International Somali Awards 2019. London, England. Courtesy of ISA

Part Five
AWARDS & SPEECH

IMAGE 19:
The author Abdulahi Haji reporting from Buckingham Palace in London 1981.
Courtesy of Farhan Jimale @farhanjimale https://x.com/farhanjimale

IMAGE 20:
The author Abdulahi Haji reporting from Buckingham Palace in London 1981.
Courtesy of BBC Webarchives https://www.bbc.co.uk/webarchive

Abdullahi Haji
My Life Through News Media

IMAGE 21:
From left to right: The author Abdulahi Haji, late BBC journalist Abdirisak Haji Mohamed Sirad, and BBC journalist Farhan Jimale.
Courtesy of Farhan Jimale https://www.facebook.com/farhan.jimale

IMAGE 22:
Abdullahi Haji, Mustafa Shafi, Abdinur Sheikh, Shamsa Abdullahi, Mohamed Abdullahi, Said Ali Musse, Mohamed Rashid Sheikh Hassan, Philippa Joy, Mohamed Hamu Sheikh
Seated: Yonis Ali Nur, Adan Nuh Dhule, Suleiman Barkhad, Abdisalam Hereri.
Location: Bush House, London
Courtesy of BBC Somali https://www.bbc.com/somali/war-40601558

Part Five
Awards & Speech

IMAGE 23:
From left to right, starting at those standing: , the author Abdulahi Haji, and . Seated are from left to right: ., and
Courtesy of BBC Somali https://www.bbc.co.uk/news/av/world-africa-40638453

IMAGE 24:
Nur Shire Osman, Ahmed Said Egeh, Ahmed Hassan Awke, Abdisalam Hereri, Yonis Ali Nur, Adan Nuh Dhule.
Seated: Abdinur Sheikh Mohamed Isahaq, Said Ali Muse.

IMAGE 25:
From left to right, Farhan Jimale, Mowlid Haji, the author Abdulahi Haji, and Mohamed Adde.
London, 2017.
Courtesy of https://x.com/BBCSomali

IMAGE 26:
From left to right, the author Abdulahi Haji, and Yusuf Garaad
London, 2025.
Courtesy of Yusuf Garaad

Part Five
AWARDS & SPEECH

IMAGE 27:

Hassan Isse Jama
Courtesy of BBC Somali

IMAGE 28:

Said Farah Mahamud
Courtesy of BBC Somali

IMAGE 31:

Abdirisaq Haji M. Sirad
Courtesy of BBC Somali

IMAGE 32:

Mohamud Hassan
Courtesy of BBC Somali

Abdullahi Haji
My Life Through News Media

IMAGE 33:
From left to right, Yusuf Garaad and the author Abdulahi Haji.
New Broadcasting House.
Courtesy of Yusuf Garaad

IMAGE 34:
From left to right, Yusuf Garaad and the author Abdulahi Haji.
London.
Courtesy of Yusuf Garaad

IMAGE 35:
Abdullahi Haji, Abdinur Sheikh, Yusuf Garaad.
Location: New Broadcasting House
Courtesy of Yusuf Garaad

IMAGE 33:
Abdullahi Haji, three BBC colleagues - not members of the Somali Service, Yusuf Garaad, Kati Mohamed Isse Trunji, Abdinur Sheikh, Daud Aweis - currently Minister of Information of the Federal Government of Somalia.
New Broadcasting House.
Courtesy of Yusuf Garaad

Part Five
Awards & Speech

IMAGE 34
Bush House, 1993.
Yusuf - Garaad, Mohamud Hassan, Florence Akst (Head BBC Somali Service), Abdullahi Haji, Abdinur Sheikh, Shamsa Abdullahi, Aden Nuh Dhule.

IMAGE 35
Left to right: Broadcaster, and publisher Abdiaziz "Xildhibaan" and the author Abdullahi Haji.

BIBLIOGRAPHY

Abdi Yusuf (May 2019): BBC Somali Service; Journalists Struggling With Their Own Language. Wardheernews. Available: https://wardheernews.com/bbc-somali-service-journalists-struggling-with-their-own-language/. Accessed: 10 April 2024.

BBC (1920): History of the BBC. Available: https://www.bbc.com/historyofthebbc/timelines/1920s. Accessed: 09 June 2024.

BBC (18 October 1922): The formation of the BBC. Available: https://www.bbc.com/historyofthebbc/anniversaries/october/formation-of-the-bbc. Accessed: 12 June 2024.

BBC (November 2011): The Media of Somalia: A Force for Moderation? Available: https://downloads.bbc.co.uk/worldservice/trust/pdf/bbc_world_service_trust_pb4_english_web.pdf. Accessed; 03 August 2024.

BBC News (14 May 2020): Somalia's coronavirus khat bans leaves chewers in a stew

Published. Available: https://www.bbc.co.uk/news/world-africa-52629112

Barker, Martin, & Petley, Julian, eds (2001), Ill Effects: The media/violence debate – Second edition, London: Routledge

Chomsky, Noam & Herman, Edward S. (1988, 2002). Manufacturing Consent: The Political Economy of the Mass Media. New York: Pantheon

Diana Njeru (2025): How how radio is helping improve health in Kenya. Available: https://www.bbc.co.uk/mediaaction/publications-and-resources/my-media-action-films/africa/kenya/diana-njeru. Accessed; 21/07/2025.

Bibliography

Durham, M. & Kellner, D. 2001: Media and Cultural Studies. UK: Blackwell Publishing Gauntlett, David (2005), Moving Experiences – Second Edition: Media Effects and Beyond, London: John Libbey

Issa-Salwe Abdisalam 1996: The Collapse of the Somali State: the Impact of Colonial Legacy. Han Associate Publisher.

_____. (2008): The Internet and the Somali Diaspora: The Web as a new means of expression. Bildhaan, 6, 1–14.

McCombs, M; Shaw, D.L. (1972 "The Agenda-setting Function of the Mass Media". Public Opinion Quarterly. 36 (2): 176–187. doi:10.1086/267990.

McLuhan Marshall (1964): The Medium Is The Massage Summary: The Impact of Media on Human Perception and Society.

Nabi, Robin L., and Mary B. Oliver. The SAGE Handbook of Media Processes and Effects. SAGE, 2009.

New York Times (July 20, 1982): Opinion: The Saddest War. Available : https://www.nytimes.com/1982/07/20/opinion/the-saddest-war.html. Accessed: 12 April 2024.

Radio Mogadishu Archive (13 February 2024): Radio Mogadishu: Saving History for the Future. Available: https://unsdg.un.org/latest/stories/radio-mogadishu-saving-history-future#:~:text=Radio%20Mogadishu%20was%20first%20established,Somali%20p ro gramming%20followed%20soon%20afterwards. (UN Sustainable Development Group. Accessed 14 May 2024.

Walter J. Ong, (1982): Orality and Literacy: The Technologizing of the Word. London: Methuen, Available: https://newlearningonline.com/literacies/chapter-1/ong-on-the-differences-between-orality-and-literacy, pp.31, 37-49.

World Day for Audiovisual Heritage: Somalia's treasure lies in Radio Mogadishu

2012 Radio Mogadishu Archive. Available: https://moi.gov.so/ova_dep/rm/. Accessed: 09 April 2024

UNSOM (21 October 2023): Radio Mogadishu: Saving Historic Audio Recordings For Future Generations Of Somalis. United Nations Assistance Mission in Somalia. Available: https://unsom.unmissions.org/radio-mogadishu-saving-historic-audio- recordings-future-generations-somalis. Accessed 19 April 2024.

INDEX

A

Abdikarim Ali 88
Abdirahman Abby Farah xiv
Abdirashid Ali Sharmarke 37
Abdirashid Duale 101
Abdi Yusuf 24, 25, 129
Abdullahi Abdi 06
Abdulqadir Shire 53
Abyssinian 91
Adam Osman 77
Adan Jama 98, 108
Addis Ababa 06, 07, 73, 74, 75, 76, 77
Addis Ababa Radio 06
Africa 15, 22, 33, 47, 53, 74, 82, 88, 89, 109
African BBC Service xiii, 11
Ahmednur Mohamed Farah 50, 51
Ahmed Sheekh xiv, xxiv, 98, 107
Ali Darwish 88
Al Jazeera 45, 51
AllAfrica.com 20
Al-Shabab 33, 34, 35, 36, 45, 47, 49
Ambo Agricultural College 06
Amharic xvi, 04, 06, 22
Arabian Peninsula 97
Arab Republic of Yemen 88, 89
Asnake 81
Australia 110
Awaday 90

B

BBC xiii, xv, xvi, xvii, xxiii, xxiv, 07, 08, 09, 11, 12, 13, 14, 17, 19, 20, 21, 23, 24, 25, 32, 34, 35, 36, 41, 42, 45, 47, 48, 49, 50, 51, 54, 86, 111, 129
BBC Somali Service xiii, xv, xvi, xvii, xxiii, 07, 11, 13, 19, 24, 25, 111, 129
BBC World Service 13, 14, 19, 21, 50, 51, 111
Bishoftu 04
Bole International Airport 74
Britain 81, 93
British Government 14, 112
British Somaliland 38
Burton 92
Burundi 89

C

California 79, 97
Cardiff 94
Catha edulis 88, 89, 109
cathine 93, 94
Cathinone 93, 94
Cathinone H. D 93

Index

'Ceelasha Biyaha 100
Chandler 54
Chatham Island 12
C. J. Martin 07, 08
Class C drug 94

CMC 52, 64
CNN 12
Col. Mengistu 74, 75, 78
Cologne 07
Columbus 96

D

Dagahbur 39, 80
Dahabshiil 100
Dahlgren 54
Daudi Aweis 36
DEA 96, 97, 110
Debrezet 04
Defence Minister Ali Ismail Yaqub 40
Deuze 55, 56
Dhagahbur 03
Diaspora 21, 23, 100, 130

Dickens 04
Dire Dawa 79, 80
Djibouti 20, 89, 90, 102
Dr. Abdi Aden 77
Dr. Hawo 100
Dr. Manton Hirst 109
'Drs. Hawo Abdi Foundation 100
Drug Enforcement Administration 96, 110
Dr. Yassin 98, 107

E

East Africa 53, 86, 88, 89, 96, 97
East and West 07
Eastern Congo 89
Eastern Hararghe's Health Administration 81
Eastern Highlands 94
Emperor Haile Selassie 04, 37, 81
EPRDF 74, 75, 76, 78, 80, 81

Ethiopia 04, 07, 08, 13, 20, 36, 37, 38, 40, 73, 77, 78, 79, 80, 81, 82, 86, 89, 90, 91, 95, 96, 101, 102
Ethiopian Air Force 04
Ethiopian Empire 36
Ethiopians 08, 40, 41, 76, 93
Europe 52, 81, 91, 96

F

Florence Akst 73

G

Garissa 25
Gatwick 94
General Post Office 14, 112

General Teferre Benti 75
Germany 06, 07
Ghion Hotel 74, 77

Guglielmo Marconi 15

H

Hadow 79
Haile Selassie Intermediate School 04
Haji Farah Hayd, 03
Harar 03, 04, 05, 79, 89, 90, 91, 92
Heathrow Airport 73, 94

Heegan 53
Hodayo 40
Holland 91
Hollywood 79
Horn of Africa 12, 19, 88, 89, 96
Hugh Walker xiv
Hussein Mohamed Bullale, 08

I

Ibnu Fadlillahi Al-Amiri 91
International Court of Justice 87
International Somali Awards xiv, 99

Issa-Salwe viii, xiv, xv, xxiv, 12, 21, 53, 54, 55, 56, 57, 58, 64, 130

J

Jigjiga 79, 80, 81
John Wilkinson 11

Jon Wilkins xiii

K

Karamardha Mountains 79
Kasmo 53, 110
Kenya xvii, 25, 37, 86, 87, 89, 90, 91, 94, 95, 96, 102, 129
Kenyan Agriculture Minister Peter Munya 87
Khalid Macow 53

khat 82, 83, 84, 85, 86, 87, 88, 89, 90, 91, 92, 93, 94, 95, 96, 97, 98, 99, 101, 102, 107, 110, 129
Khat 84, 86, 88, 89, 90, 94, 95, 96, 98, 102, 103, 107, 108, 110
Khoisan 109
Kimathi Munjuri 87
Kismayo 34

L

Lancaster's South-Eastern Correctional Institution 96

Latin Somali language alphabet 33

Index

Leninist 75
Liberation Front 40, 78

London xiv, xxiv, 07, 08, 11, 13, 19, 23, 45, 47, 53, 78, 93, 94, 95, 98, 107, 110, 129, 130

M

Makhtal Dahir 40
Makka 92
Malawi 89
Manchester 94
Marxist 74, 75
McLuhan 12, 15, 43, 64, 130
McQuail 55, 57, 58
Meles Zenawi 77, 78, 82
Mengistu Haile Mariam 37, 74
Mero 90
Middle East 53, 96, 97
Midlands 94
Minister of Information 06
Ministry of Information 06, 07

Ministry of Information, 06, 07
miraa 87, 94
Missing Relative Session 13
Misuse of Drugs Act 1971 94
Mogadishu viii, 07, 09, 15, 22, 36, 38, 45, 72, 80, 86, 87, 90, 95, 100, 130
Mohamed Abdi-Daud 91
Mohamed Kooreeye 98, 108
Mohamed Mohamoud 99, 108
Mohamed Siyad Barre 09, 90, 94
Mr. Jama 99, 108
Mr. Mohamoud 99

N

Nairobi xv, xvii, 19, 25
National Board of Health and Welfare 88
National Committee for the Eradication of Khat. 83
National Criminal Intelligence Service 93
National Union of Somali Journalists 50
NCIS 93, 94, 110

Newsweek 95, 96, 110
Newsweek's 92
New York Times 41, 130
New Zealand 110
North-east 94
Northeastern Kenya 20
Northern Opposition Group 38
North-west 94
NUSOJ 50

O

Ogaden 36, 37, 38, 39, 40, 41, 79, 80, 81
Ogaden liberation movements 38

Ogaden region 36, 37, 38, 39, 40
Ogaden war 36
Ogaden War 37, 80

Ohio 96
OLF 78
Omar Qadi 51
Ong 65, 66, 130
Oromo 22, 40, 78
Oromos 78, 101, 102

Osman Hassan 08
Osman Sugulle 08
Osob Mohamed Hayd 03
Ottoman 92
Ottoman Empire 92

P

Pacific 12
Peoples Revolutionary Democratic Front 74
President Hassan Sheekh 86

President Mohamed Abdullahi Farmajo 86, 87
President Uhuru Kenyatta 86
Professor Said Samatar 12

Q

Qu'ran 92, 102

Quutul awliya 92

R

Radio Hargeisa 36
Radio Mogadishu 22, 130, 131
Radio Xurmo 36
Republic of Somaliland 38

Revolutionary Council 75
Richard Burton 91
Riyadh 97, 110
Robert Park 55

S

Sahra Abdi 45, 50
Samarqandi. Kilwa 91
Saudi Arabia 91, 110
Scotland 94
Shabelle Media Network 20
Shakespeare 04
Sheikh Abadir Muse 92
Sheikh Abdulla 92
Sheikh Sufi Quranic school 03
Siyad Barre 22, 33, 37, 38

Somalia viii, 07, 08, 11, 13, 15, 19, 20, 21, 22, 23, 24, 25, 31, 32, 33, 34, 36, 37, 38, 39, 40, 41, 45, 47, 48, 49, 50, 53, 66, 71, 72, 80, 86, 87, 88, 89, 90, 94, 96, 97, 100, 102, 109, 110, 129, 131
Somali Media Sector 47
Somali National TV 23
Somali Republic 36, 38, 39
Somali Revolutionary Party 53
Somali Swedish Development and Relief Association 88

Index

Somali Women in Sweden 88
South Africa 88, 89, 109
South Central Somalia 36, 67

Supreme Revolutionary Council 09
Sweden 88, 91

T

Tanzania 89

Transitional Federal Government 45

U

Uganda 89
Uhuru Kenyatta 87
UNDP 34
United Kingdom 91, 94
United Nations 22, 38, 87, 131

United Nations Sustainable Development Group 22
United Nations trusteeship 22
United States 74, 91, 92, 95, 96, 97, 110